I Got Shoes

A Memoir

JAMES L. LIPSCOMB

On The Hill, LLC

Scottsdale, Arizona 85262

ISBN: 978-1-7320-0190-9 (sc)
ISBN: 978-1-7320-0191-6 (hc)
ISBN: 978-1-7320-0192-3 (e)

Library of Congress Control Number: 2018907054

rev. date: 07/27/2018

In memory of my mother and father, who gave life to fourteen children in Coeymans. To my wife, Nancy, who brought me my new beginning in life. To my children (Kathy, Julie and Angela), my grandchildren, and their progeny. May this short trip down memory lane preserve a portion of your heritage. In memory of the Negro people of Coeymans, New York, from 1925 to 1962, who are not in our history books but remain in my heart and mind. In memory of my cousin and best friend, McKinley Jones Jr., who reminded us all that "something good can come out of Coeymans."

CONTENTS

PREFACE

The Coeymans, New York, of my childhood is a bygone era that exists in name only today. While there is some history of Coeymans, there is little or no history of the Negro in Coeymans in the 1900s. The Negroes were migrants and recruits from Virginia and the Carolinas in search of work on the brickyards along the Hudson River in New York State. Although some had their remains returned to the South, Grove Cemetery in Coeymans is the final resting place for the remains of many former Negro inhabitants. Unfortunately, they can no longer relate their history for posterity. In this book, I bring to life not only the physical place but also many of the people who lived in Coeymans in a bygone era. I share little known events, the joys and pains of life, the people's relationships, unforgettable experiences, and my personal feelings. In this regard, there are a number of stories to be told.

My experience growing up in Coeymans became the impetus for my desire for a college education. Most of the adults I knew while growing up in Coeymans never finished high school, and while most of their children did finish high school, few if any went to college. Getting and keeping a job was given priority over going to college. In this book, I trace my childhood history beyond Coeymans to Albany and on to college and through law school. Apart from a constant struggle, there was a broadening of my worldview that intensified my desire for a better life. My broader education happened in both my academic and living environments at the same time. I put in this book those stories that I regard as memorable parts of my life journey. They have obviously provided lasting impressions for me. To the extent my journey has intersected with the lives of others, I respect their rights to recall those events as they know and believe them to have been.

Over my years, the way in which my race has been viewed in the United States and indeed the world has changed many times. In this book, I have made one small gesture in regard to these changes. I begin the book referring to people of my race as "Negroes" and then "black people." It was not until after the time period of this book that black people in the United States started to be referred to as "African Americans." I have spent my whole life trying not to see people as a member of a particular race but rather as individuals who happen to be of one ethnicity or another. The treatments in this book represent the environments of the times in which I grew up and not a change in my personal view. I remain a believer in the individual character of everyone and the need to see everyone in their respective individual capacities irrespective of their ethnic heritage.

To provide perspective, I divided the book along five-year intervals, all of which are approximate and not intended to be precise. The titles to the chapters are intended to suggest the mood of the particular time period. Each segment is intended to convey stories of my life but not necessarily every story. Choosing to relate one story versus another is the product of my best recollection at the moment, personal experience, and selecting the story that makes the desired point. Given more time, I am sure that I would add or drop a few stories for the same reasons.

I could have called this book *The Boy from Coeymans*, given the significant influence my experience in Coeymans has had on my life. There are many men from Coeymans who could have rightfully claimed that title over time. I chose *I Got Shoes* because the title goes deeper into my experience, invokes my religious upbringing, and presents me today as an able man on many dimensions of life. Although this book stops short of the beginning of my professional life, it provides a unique perspective of the platform upon which my professional life has been built.

ACKNOWLEDGMENTS

For the most part, the events in this book took place prior to fifty years ago. While I recall specific events, I am grateful to my brother John Henry Lipscomb for his assistance with the recollections of events and the names of specific people in Coeymans. I am also grateful to my daughter Kathryn Lipscomb Strahs for her help with the genealogy and history of my descendants. I also appreciate the comments from my brother Eugene, my friend Will Frager and my wife Nancy, all of whom reviewed drafts of this book.

INTRODUCTION

I Shall Remember You Lois

The rain was coming down at a steady pace in the Indian summer of September 1950. I could see it sheeting off the eaves of the roof. We lived in the ground-floor flat of a two-story company house that had a tin roof and no gutters. The rain formed puddles along the sides of the house and little streams ran away from the house to the ditch along the vegetable garden. It was raining when I got up that morning, and it had not stopped.

I was waiting for everyone to come back. I didn't know then where they had gone. All I knew was that some of my older brothers and sisters went with my mother and father in two black cars with a white man. Green and Francis Motley, my aunt and uncle who lived in the flat upstairs, followed behind them in their car. Nobody in my family knew how to drive, and we didn't own a car.

"De comin'!" somebody yelled. We all ran to the windows to watch the cars as they turned into our driveway, an earthen path with gravel on top. It was muddy, and the puddles were everywhere. Slowly, the cars approached, attempting to get as close to the house as possible. There was no front porch, just a wide plank in front of the door. When the cars stopped, the doors opened slowly, and everyone seemed to get out at the same time. Notwithstanding the rain, they seemed to be moving slowly. Then I noticed my mother. Despite the rain, I could see the tears coming down her face. She could hardly move. Everyone seemed to be lending her a hand to get into the house. One by one, they entered the house and stood in the middle of the living room. It seemed as if everyone was sad, and many were crying except my father. He looked somewhat tired. I wanted to ask what was wrong; however, I was scared, and I started to cry as well. I don't know why. I imagine it was because everyone seemed so sad.

It wasn't until several days later that I realized my sister Lois was not coming home. I have only a faint memory of Lois. She was only about three years old—the next-youngest child after me. She never did walk or talk as a child, even when she was old enough to be walking and talking. No one ever told me what was wrong with Lois, but I believe it would be diagnosed today as polio. She slept in a yellow wrought iron crib that had rockers at both ends. My mother and others in the family would rock her in the crib. Sometimes she would just cry, and everyone seemed helpless.

One day she was no longer in the crib, and I didn't know where she had gone. Everyone seemed to whisper, and they all had pale looks on their faces. I remember them talking about "Babcock," whom I later came to know as the local funeral director. Now they had returned, and everyone was crying. Ma was standing in the kitchen crying, and John Henry, my oldest living brother, was standing next to her and holding her hand. Lois was now gone forever—at least in this life. She was the eleventh child in a family of twelve children. (Carol and Deborah were not yet born.) She was not the first to die. Thomas Eric and Rosa Mae had also died at a young age before I was born. The next day—or so it seemed—Lois's crib was set outside and eventually carried away by the junk man.

As I think about the death of Lois, I think about Coeymans and the Negro people. Some things have gone from memory, but much remains as reminders of the guideposts in my life. The Coeymans of Lois's time represents the fabric of my life. I know now, decades later, that the Coeymans I knew lives on in the lives of those who were there, and all seemed to have carried their Coeymans with them for all their days on earth. What was this place called Coeymans, and who were these people?

COEYMANS

The town of Coeymans was founded by Barent Pieteres Koijemans, who arrived from Holland in 1639 and became an apprentice at a gristmill owned by the Patron Van Rensselaer. Barent purchased land from Native Americans in 1672 that became known as the Coeymans Patent. For more than two hundred years, Coeymans was known for its family-owned gristmills. In the 1880s, the gristmills began to close and give way to the family-owned brickyards that sprung up along the Hudson River. The Powell & Minnock brick company opened in the late 1880s along with other brick companies, such as Sutton & Suderly and Roah Hook.

The Coeymans that I grew up in, the Negro community, does not exist today in terms of either physical structures or the people. There are some residual structures that have been repurposed, but most have been torn down. The housing, places of employment, food supply, and people of my time are nearly all gone. The one remaining vestige of the Negro community of my time is the Riverview Missionary Baptist Church. It is for this reason that I feel compelled to bring the former Negro community back to life and provide an opportunity for its prior existence to be memorialized in some limited way. History will little note or long remember the Negro population of the Coeymans of my time. This book will be one of the few markers in remembrance.

The Lay of the Land

Once again, I find myself awake at the crack of dawn. It must be about five o'clock. Daddy has gone to work. He usually goes to the brickyard about three thirty in the morning. He gets an early start so he can get home early—usually around ten thirty in the morning or so. Ma gets up when he gets up and stays up. She already has a pot of coffee (hot water over coffee grounds that boil over into the coffee itself and thickens the longer the pot sits on the fire) on the stove. The pot sits on a woodstove that throws off a lot of heat even when you don't need it, particularly in the summertime.

Everyone else seems to be asleep, but I know they are just trying to stay in bed until the last possible moment. I'll be glad when the day comes that I can have my own room and my own bed. Pearl, Janet, Linda, and Deborah are in one bed, and Clifford, Gene, and I are in the other bed, all in the same room. German is sleeping in a small closet behind a curtain in the hall. Sally and Mary Lee are in the next room, where we have our main woodstove for heating and where we have the dining room table. John Henry left home some time ago and now lives in Newburgh and works at West Point as an orderly.

It is June, and we don't have school until September. As I sit here waiting for the sun, as well as the people in the house to really get up, I think about my part of Coeymans. Coeymans is a small hamlet about thirteen miles south of Albany, New York, on Route 144, the main road from the north on my side of town. As you enter town, there are eight company houses. We call this area the Hill. Continuing along Route 144 down the Hill, on the left side is the entrance to the Sutton & Suderly Brick

Company (the brickyard) and John and Susie Moten's house. On the right side of Route 144, down in a valley, is the Bottom because of its location at the foot of the Hill. In the winter we ride sleighs from the top of the Hill down into the Bottom. There are about seven houses down in the Bottom. All of them are company houses except the one owned by the Whittakers.

The local bar, Adamo's (operated by Joe Adamo), is located at the foot of the Hill just beyond the Bottom. The primary patrons of the bar are the Negro men in the community, including many who work on the brickyard but live in Albany. A few paces down the road from Adamo's and across the street is John Henry Thomas Brewer's house. The house is located at the beginning of a concrete bridge over Coeymans Creek. At the end of the bridge is the right turn that takes you to Riverview Missionary Baptist Church and the Frangella mushroom plant. It is hard to believe that a stinky old mushroom plant is allowed next door to a church. No one talks about it aloud. It seems that everyone in the church is connected in some way to the Frangellas and related families (Adamo, Pape, and Mayone). No one would risk stirring up trouble with those employers.

Also at the corner of the bridge is a house occupied by Wildy and Willie Lee Pounds on the top floor and Sally and LeRoy Fordham on the ground floor. One day while picking wild strawberries in the woods in back of this house, we found the grave site of the Coeymans family—the Dutch founders of the hamlet. Also along the church road is the house of Albert Nino, an Italian man who works as a local housepainter. Mr. Nino is such a meticulous painter. Having observed the way he painted, I knew that I wanted to paint like him.

Continuing along Route 144 a short distance, there is Mayone's grocery, where most people of the Negro community buy their groceries, usually on credit. Andrew and Julia Mayone live upstairs above the store with their two sons, Peter and Andrew Jr. Across the street from Mayone's is the Legg family. They live in a very small house that seems hardly big enough for the family. In back of the Legg family home is the continuation of Coeymans Creek as it turns into a small waterfall over the rocks. We refer to this area as the Sucker Hole because of the trout-like fish that we catch there.

Continuing along Route 144 for about one-tenth of a mile, you come to a fork in the road. The right prong of the fork is Church Street, but we referred to it as Altimari's Hill because an old Italian man named Tommy Altimari lives adjacent to the hill and because his brother Mike Altimari lives at the left prong of the fork in the road, where he operates a bar and grill. Negroes seldom go there. There was talk that a Negro man was poisoned in the bar. Down Route 144 a few houses from Mike's place are the law offices of Edward Uthe, a prominent lawyer in town. People refer to him as Judge Uthe (or Judge Juicy) because he used to be a justice of the peace. Judge Uthe is a heavyset, white-haired white man with very distinguished features. He usually wears a three-piece suit, white shirt, and a bow tie, and he looks important. Each year he sponsors a trip for all the kids in town who want to go to Hawkins Stadium in Albany to see a minor league baseball game. He gives each kid fifty cents for soda and hot dogs. At Easter, he also sponsors the giveaway of Easter baskets to kids at the Coeymans elementary school.

At the corner of the Uthe building is the left turn on 4th Street to go down to the church parsonage situated on 1st Street at the foot of the hill next door to another mushroom-growing room owned by the Frangellas. Across the street from the parsonage is the home of Arthur and Eva Leigh. The Leighs are prominent members of the church. They have four grown children—Little Arthur, Geneva, Fanny, and Eugene. Geneva is the mother of my best friend, Tony Kittle, who also lives in the house.

Continuing on Route 144 for a few more houses, you come to the post office. This is where everyone comes to pick up their mail. We have box 74 with a combination lock on it. There is no home delivery of mail. Next door to the post office on the north is a pale green house with shuttered windows where an elderly man lives. We call him Grover, but we do not know his real name. He is thin, and he wears an odd-looking hat, a long beard, and round rimless glasses. Although he has never bothered or spoken to us, we are afraid to walk by his house, particularly if he is outside. Next door to the post office on the south is Pape's Confectionery Store, the candy store. Mrs. Pape is an elderly Italian lady who lives on the premises with her daughters. Next door to Pape's on the south is Cappolarello's grocery. The Cappolarellos are also an elderly Italian couple who also live on the premises. When we walk to school, rather than going up Altimari's Hill, we go down by Pape's and Cappolarello's for candy and then take a side path opposite the post office up the hill to continue on to school. On our way home from school, we sometimes retrace our steps in order to stop for Popsicles.

Route 144 continues on down past Bruno's newsstand, where people come to get the newspapers and to catch the bus either north to Albany or to points south of Coeymans. At the corner of Bruno's is the left turn on to Westerlo Street to go to Pape's grocery store (locally referred to as Chubbys, after the physique of the owner Carmino Pape). This is at the far end of town and is not frequented by Negroes. Route 144 continues on along the Hudson River into a hamlet called New Baltimore and eventually connects to Route 9W, which goes south toward Coxsackie and New York City.

COEYMANS, NEW YORK 1925-1961
The Negro Community

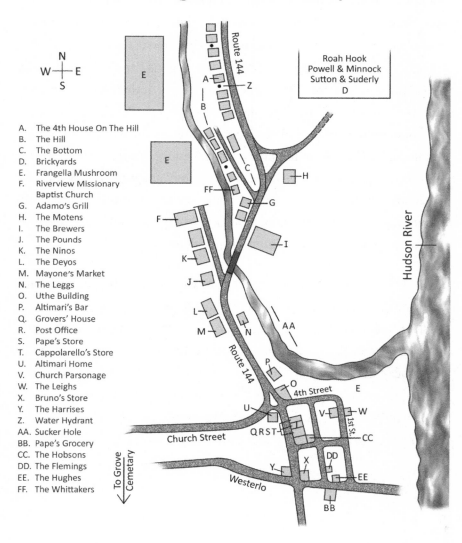

A. The 4th House On The Hill
B. The Hill
C. The Bottom
D. Brickyards
E. Frangella Mushroom
F. Riverview Missionary
   Baptist Church
G. Adamo's Grill
H. The Motens
I. The Brewers
J. The Pounds
K. The Ninos
L. The Deyos
M. Mayone's Market
N. The Leggs
O. Uthe Building
P. Altimari's Bar
Q. Grovers' House
R. Post Office
S. Pape's Store
T. Cappolarello's Store
U. Altimari Home
V. Church Parsonage
W. The Leighs
X. Bruno's Store
Y. The Harrises
Z. Water Hydrant
AA. Sucker Hole
BB. Pape's Grocery
CC. The Hobsons
DD. The Flemings
EE. The Hughes
FF. The Whittakers

The Negro Community

As Coeymans evolved from the gristmill economy to the brickyards, the population shifted as well. The largely Italian population in the north end of Coeymans moved as the brickyard companies sought cheaper labor. Some brickyard owners went south to Virginia and the Carolinas to recruit Negro labor. The Italians had come from Europe, where unions were strong. The brickyard owners preferred the cheaper nonunion labor of the Negroes. Negroes agreeing to come to Coeymans could live in company housing. The adult Negro population in Coeymans lived through World War I, the Great Depression, and World War II. Coeymans is largely a segregated hamlet, with most of the Negroes living at the north end of town, either on the Hill or in the Bottom, sandwiched between the brickyard and the mushroom plant. Others live on the north side of the Coeymans Creek Bridge. One or two, the Leighs, the Flemings and the Hobsons, live on the south end near the church parsonage. Many of the Negro families in Coeymans followed others north in search of a better life. The Negro community has about 250 residents, and everyone knows one another, including all the children. While there is familiarity, there is also formality. Adults are always addressed as Mr. or Mrs., except for a curious development where some of the men are addressed by their first name (or nickname) preceded by Mr. and some of the adult women are called by their first name (or nickname) preceded by Miss. For example, Mrs. Dicey Wilson is called Miss Dicey, and Mr. Hughes, whose first name is Whitfield, is called Mr. Teevey.

In many ways, virtually everyone in the Negro community is related either by blood or marriage at various levels of ancestry. When they aren't related, they are close enough in friendship to be family. This is not to say that everyone is friendly with one another. Such is not the case. There are lines of division, particularly among the adults. While no one is wealthy by the standards of white people, some families have a few pennies more than others and act like it is more than a few pennies. Some families regularly attend church, and some do not. Some have a lot of children, and some have only a few. Children have their differences— sometimes related to the differences of their parents and sometimes not. Some get invited to weddings, and some do not. Most go to funerals, and a few do not. If you go to church, you have to wear your Sunday best, or you do not go. Even so, some are the subject of many whispers and laughs by those who think the attire is less than appropriate.

The Negro community is a transplant of the way of life in the South. The people follow many of the customs and the activities that characterized their lives in the South. They come from an agrarian society and spend considerable effort in their gardens to raise foodstuff to help make ends meet. They also raise pigs, chickens, and other animals for food, as well as fish and hunt wild animals such as rabbits, squirrels, deer, and pheasants. The women use home remedies for illnesses rather than visiting the doctor. While the social life has the church at its core, it nevertheless includes men and women engaging in improper social conduct, including extramarital affairs. No one talks openly about such conduct, but everyone seems to be aware of such activities. In the extreme, some of the people are suspected of practicing voodoo in the hopes of impacting the lives of their neighbors.

Everything and everyone in the Negro community is within walking distance. Nonetheless, those with cars make sure they wash them and take them to church even if the car motor does not warm up in the time it takes to get to church. Some of the children have bicycles and tricycles. However, for the most part, the people walk.

Because the community is small, everyone knows everyone else. Unfortunately, some also feel it appropriate to know everyone's business as well and do not hesitate to share whatever they *know* about someone else. Doors have locks, but since someone is always home, locks are rarely used except at night. You do not need to be invited to most of the homes, particularly if you are a child. However, as a child, you never stay for a meal unless invited and then only if you check with your mother first. At Christmas and New Year's, everyone seems to have an open door, and it is expected that people will stop by for a drink and social conversation. The men have made it a tradition—the drinking being one tradition that many of the women wish would hurry up and pass.

The Hill

The Sutton & Suderly Brick Company provides company housing (formerly occupied by Italian families that lived and worked in the area) on the Hill and in the Bottom for the Negro workers. The white workers at the brickyard have the higher-paying jobs and live in other parts of Coeymans and Ravena. All but two of the houses are painted a bluish gray with white trim. It would be an overstatement to say the houses have been painted because I cannot recall ever seeing anyone paint any of the houses. The houses do not have electricity, water, or sewer. Kerosene lamps are used to light the houses. Water is carried by pails from a common hydrant, and outhouses sit just in back. Over the years electricity has been added to some houses by running wires to place a single socket in the middle of each room for a light. When a family is able to afford a refrigerator instead of the icebox, an extension cord is run from the ceiling light to the refrigerator.

The northernmost house, the eighth house, situated on Route 144 on the north side of Coeymans, is occupied by the Stevens family. Mitchell and Lena Stevens have been in Coeymans for many years. Lena is a fair-skinned, portly built woman with gray hair and green eyes. She works as a housekeeper for white people in Coeymans and Ravena. Mr. Mitchell is a tall, dark-skinned, slender man with a thin mustache. He wears suspenders and often smokes a stogie cigar and sometimes a pipe. It's not unusual for him to send plumes of smoke into the air, and it behooves you to stand away when speaking with him to avoid the smell and the smoke. He works on the brickyard. The Stevens have several children, some of whom married locally. David Stevens married Helen Sutton, the daughter of Pastor Sutton. Mitchell Jr. (Mick) married Inez Brewer, the daughter of John Henry and Bernice Brewer. Their grandson Billy Stevens (son of their daughter Virginia), one of my best friends, lives with them. They have several other children, namely Edward and Shirley, who are also married, and there's also Gertrude and Catherine, who are not married. Catherine is an excellent cook and probably the best aunt any best friend could have. She buys Billy everything he wants, or so it seems.

Mr. Mitchell does not say much to children, but sometimes he teases us. He has a lot of farm equipment, including several tractors. He plows up several acres of land north of his property for a variety of crops. His son Mick plows up land for gardens for the others in the community who pay a fee.

The seventh house on the Hill used to be occupied by Sarah and Yancy Hughes, the parents of Whitfield "Teevy" Hughes. Miss Sarah, as she was called, was one of my mother's best friends. Although old enough to be my mother's mother, Miss Sarah often came to visit my mother, and my mother went to visit her. Her untimely passing was devastating to my mother. Mr. Yancy soon moved away, and the house is now occupied by the Gladney family.

James Gladney and his brother Edward (Willie) came from the South. They are known as Lightning and Thunder, respectively, largely because of their strength and daredevil reputation. Lightning, a tall, heavyset man, married Etta Walton, and they have several children (Jimmy, Loretta, Bonnie, Eartha, Eddie, Jerry, and Barbara). He seems to work all the time, having both a day job and a night job. Jimmy, his son, is also one of my best friends. They, too, have a garden near the house where they grow vegetables. In addition, they raise pigs and chickens. Water for the house comes from a hydrant that sits between the seventh house and the sixth house.

The sixth house on the Hill is occupied by the Walton family. William and Cornelia Walton have a large family. They have several girls (Ollie, May, Etta, Ruthie, Virginia, and Louise) and one son, William (Bill). Mr. William works on the brickyard. Miss Walton works in Albany as a housekeeper. Miss Walton is the sister of Bernice Brewer, the wife of John Henry Thomas Brewer, who lives near the Coeymans Bridge. Oddly, both of them are addressed by their married names Miss Walton and Miss Brewer. Mr. William also has a garden as well as several chickens and pigs. I recall the time Mr. William claimed to have grown tomatoes on his potato vines. It did happen. I saw them, but no one knows how it happened. Mr. William seems to always be less than sober. He seems to go from the brickyard to Adamo's bar and then home. When he walks, he crosses one leg in front of the other and often steps backward. It seems to take him twice as long to arrive at his destination.

Fifth House On The Hill

The fifth house on the Hill is now occupied by the Ernest and Sylvester Ray. George Reddy used to live in the house before he died. It is one of the two houses that have different siding than all the rest. The house has white slatelike material in large sheets as siding. It also has indoor plumbing and electrical outlets.

The front porch is screened in. The front yard has a white picket fence that encloses the yard. The driveway has white stagecoach wagon wheels on either side. They also have a garage for their car. The backyard is neatly landscaped and has a picnic table and brick barbeque pit. Earnest and Sylvester Ray have two children, Charles and Leatrice. Mr. Ray works on the brickyard and his wife, Miss Sylvester, worked as a housekeeper at one point for the Suderlys and now in Albany. Mr. Ray loves fishing and often goes fishing with some of the men and older boys. Miss Sylvester is a religious woman who regularly attends Wilborne Temple in Albany. She attends church virtually all day on weekends and sometimes at night during the week. From time to time, she brings my mother some *blessed oil* from the church.

The Rays have grandchildren who come to visit from time to time. Charles and his wife, Frederica, have a son named Winston. He is a couple of years younger than me. Leatrice and her husband, James

Fourth House On The Hill

Hunt, have several children (James Jr., Gregory, Carol, Edward, and John). James Jr. (we call him Jimmy) is one of my friends. When the Hunts visit their grandmother, Jimmy gets out of the car and comes directly over to our house. When he stays with his grandparents, as he often does, Jimmy virtually lives over at our house. My mother takes care of him as if he were one of her own.

The fourth house on the Hill is a two-family house. My mother's brother Ung Green (as we call him) and his wife, Frances, live on the top floor with their children—Eva, Lenzy, Bertha, Joe, Jacob, and Elsie. (Their oldest child, Green Motley Jr., died at an early age.) We live on the ground floor. Ung Green is a handyman around the house. He put sheetrock in all the rooms in his flat. (Nearly every house has the original plaster walls.) He installed electrical outlets and built his garage, meat house, woodshed, and outhouse. He has a garden and also raises chickens and pigs. His outhouse is always neat and clean with real toilet paper.

Lilly and Howard Petersen used to live in the bottom flat of the fourth house on the Hill before moving to New York City. Miss Peterson used to prepare meals for many of the men who worked for Allegheny Steel in Waterveliet and on the brickyard, including Whiskey Bill, Blue Mountain Joe, Latin Cook, and Joe Hoss. After Ms. Petersen moved, we moved from the Bottom into the flat. We do not have sheetrock in our flat. All our walls are plastered and in need of repair. We also have several gardens and raise chickens and pigs.

In between the fourth house and the third house is a water hydrant that provides water for the first four houses on the Hill. The third house on the Hill is also a multifamily house. The Harris family occupied the top floor. The Wilson family occupied half of the first floor. And the Moore family occupied the other half. Many refer to Mr. Harris as Top because he is physically top-heavy with relatively small legs. Top and his wife, Irene, have two children, Marylyn and Maxine. Marylyn married James Wilson, who lived on the first floor. Maxine is my age. I remember not going to her birthday party because my *friends* at the time thought she liked me. They told me that her mother put *mayonnaise* on the cake for icing. Of course, the mayonnaise story was not true. I don't know about the other rumor. I sort of liked her though.

After the Harrises moved, George and Mildred Sims moved into the flat with their daughter, Bessie. After Mr. Ray died and Miss Sylvester moved to Albany, the Sims moved into the Ray's former house, and Tommy Wilson, the brother of James, and his wife Mary, now occupy the Sims's former flat.

Dan Moore (also known as Buck) and Miss Adie lived on the first floor. Miss Adie was the sister of Miss "Jenny" Hughes. Their maiden name was Brandon. Miss Adie was a favorite of my sisters Mary Lee and Pearl. She would regularly curl their hair for school and church. She would apply Dixie Peach Vaseline to their scalps and then use a hot curling iron to press the Dixie Peach into the curled hair to hold it in place. Miss Adie became very ill and went to live with Miss Jenny. We did not know her illness at the time. She looked very frail as she sat in the window at Miss Jenny's house to take in the sun. After her death we learned that she had cancer. It was the first time that I heard about cancer.

The Wilson family, which lived on the same floor as Miss Adie, expanded to the entire floor after Miss Adie went to live with her sister. Paul and Dicey Wilson have several children (Paul Jr., Mary, James, Phoebe, Anne Lee, Louise, Juanita, Leon, Florence, and Tommy), all of whom are older than me. Their oldest child, Little Paul, moved to Albany and eventually moved to California. The youngest is Tommy, who is my brother John's age. Mr. Paul works for the Sutton and Suderly brickyard in the brick dryer (commonly called the "dry" by the workers). He also has pigs, chickens, and a bull or cow from time to time. He is perhaps the best gardener in Coeymans. Before expanding into Miss Adie's space, the Wilson's kitchen was a detached building in back of the house. After the move, the kitchen became a garage and a place where Tommy repairs televisions. I learned to repair televisions while working with Tommy.

The second house on the Hill is occupied by Brummy Watkins and Alex Pointer, both single men (although Mr. Brummy had been married to Liza Watkins for a number of years) that work on the brickyard. Mr. Pointer caught tuberculosis and is spending some time in a sanatorium. Mr. Brummy is a long-time resident of Coeymans, having served in World War I. Most of the furnishings in the house belong to Mr. Brummy. He has an extensive collection of records from the 1930s and a windup Victrola record player that actually works. Mr. Brummy seems to regularly bathe with Life Buoy soap. He uses so much of it that his whole house has the smell of the soap.

The first house on the Hill is occupied by Lish Miles. It used to be occupied by Mr. Tucker and his wife, Miss Ovie, Mr. Lish's mother. Mr. Lish is a tall, lanky, fair-skinned man with a pockmarked face. He has a receding hairline, heavy eyebrows, and a gray mustache. Mr. Lish, a single man, seems to pay a lot of attention to Ann Lee Wilson, one of Mr. Paul's daughters, who lives two houses up the line. He works on the brickyard too. Rosa Logan, who lives in the Bottom, prepares his lunch pail and sometimes his supper. When he gets dressed up on weekends, he is quite a dapper-looking man.

The Bottom

The company houses in the Bottom are like the houses on the Hill - without indoor plumbing and limited electricity. The houses do not have house numbers. Nor are they referred to in any particular order. Fortunately, there is no local mail delivery to cause any confusion. The houses are adjacent to Coeymans Creek. In the spring the creek level sometimes rises to a point where the houses nearest the bank are flooded on the ground floors. The outhouses for the houses in the Bottom are on the creek bank where the waste is washed away by the waters.

The first house, which is near the base of the Hill, was occupied by Jimmy and Eva Boxley. Jimmy was one of the younger men in town who came out of the South. He married Eva Motley, Ung Green's oldest daughter. When we sleighed down the hill in the winter, we ended up in their front yard. Jimmy and Eva later moved out and subsequently divorced. Their flat later became occupied by Kelly and Blanche Banks and their son Frankie. Jimmy has since married Pearl Brewer, a daughter of John Henry and Bernice Brewer, and they reside in Coeymans. Eva has since married as well, and she resides in Albany.

The next house down on the same side nearest to Coeymans Creek is occupied by Lula Jones on the top floor and John Henry and Fannie Foy on the ground floor. Lula Jones was the wife of Sam Jones, the younger brother of my uncle McKinley Jones. Sam died suddenly in his fifties. The Joneses have five children—Sam Jr., Zelda, John Frank, Dorothy, and Bessie. Fanny is a daughter of Arthur and Eva Leigh. John and his brother Pleasant came to Coeymans from Virginia and found work on the brickyard. Fanny and John have several children, including Barbara, Gwenn, Dennis, Kenny, Michael and Johnny.

Across the road is a house that has two flats upstairs and two flats downstairs. The upstairs flats are occupied by Esau and Amelia Turner on the north and Pleasant and Zelda Jones Foy on the south. Esau also came up from the South to work on the brickyard. He married my cousin Amelia Jones, a daughter of my uncle McKinley and aunt Mary Jones. They have a daughter named Althea. Pleasant and Zelda have two children, Pleasant Jr. and Wanda. Pleasant, known to everyone as Bones because of his physical stature, is a multitalented man. He not only has a wonderful tenor voice but is talented with his hands. He can make just about anything he wants with his hands. He is also a pretty fair fine artist. Bones is an amicable man and is admired by everyone.

The downstairs flat is occupied by Corrine and Crow Toe on the north side and James and Pauline Mason on the south side. Corrine and Crow Toe are two elderly men who work around town for white people doing odd jobs. Corrine, whose real name is Bruce Moore, works for various members of the Frangella family. Sometimes he stays at their homes. Crow Toe, whose real name is William Glass, has bad feet, and one can often find him soaking them in various liniments and home remedies. His shoes do not seem to fit well, and he tends to hobble. Pauline is the daughter of Weldon Brandon, the brother of Jenny Hughes and Adie Moore. He was once a prizefighter, and he likes to be called the Champ. James and Pauline have one child named Carol.

Back across the road and along the creek bank is another two-family house. The top flat is occupied by Rosa Logan and her son Charlie. Miss Logan makes lunch pails for Mr. Brummy and Mr. Lish. My brothers John, German, and Cliff at various times carry the lunch pails to the brickyard for the men. Charlie, a rotund, fair-skinned man with bowling pin legs, is a ladies' man about town and has a reputation for not working too hard, although he does have a job on the brickyard.

Miss Nellie Mae Turner lives on the first floor, the flat we used to live in before moving to the fourth house on the Hill. Miss Nellie's husband, Garland "Teddy" Turner, was killed in a car accident on Route 9J. Marcella Anne Walton, a spunky girl my age, stays with Miss Nellie. Anne is the daughter of Virginia Walton, a daughter of Cornelia and William Walton. Miss Nellie is a short and somewhat rotund woman with small legs. She does not appear to have missed many meals. It is not uncommon to hear her complain about being hungry. "I ain't had nothing but a pound of *lasses* cookies and a pint of ice cream all day," she would say with a big smile. She is known for her prowess at fishing. Miss Nellie also has a way with words that would burn most ears.

In between where Miss Nellie lives and the next house over is a water hydrant that provides water for all the houses in the Bottom. The next house over is also a two-family house. My uncle McKinley Jones and aunt Mary live on the top floor with their children (Maxine, Sally, Aquila, Edith, Amelia, Louise, McKinley Jr., Brenda, and Jennifer). Aunt Mary is my father's sister. The ground-floor flat is occupied by the *other* Lipscomb family (said to be of no relation to my father), George and Lou Fanny. They have several children. George Jr. married Joan Hughes, the daughter of Mr. Teevy and Miss Jenny. Shirley Lipscomb married and now lives in Albany. He is well known at the local high school for his ability to play football in his younger years. Willie Lee Lipscomb married Wildy Pounds and moved to the other end of the Coeymans Creek Bridge. The two other Lipscomb children, Barbara and William, are not yet married.

The last house in the Bottom is not a company house, and it is owned by Ben and Benolier Whittaker. It is a small house that sits close to the creek bank. Miss Bee (as Benolier is called) fishes from the back of her house. They do not have any children, although James Edwards, a relative of Miss Bee, came to live with them after his discharge from the army. James subsequently married Barbara Lipscomb. Mr. Ben is also a fisherman. However, he is best known for playing cards at Adamo's. His friends call him Mr. Brisk after a card game he loved to play. Mr. Ben passed away at the card table in Adamo's with cards in his hands.

Throughout the 1940s and '50s, several families lived in the Bottom, including Grant (called Uncle Grant) and Cora Clayborn. The Bottom was at one time called Clayborn Place in honor of Uncle Grant. Uncle Grant had both of his legs amputated because of the onset of diabetes. His wife, Cora, was the sister of Mr. Mitchell, who lived in the eighth house on the Hill. The Carter family, Clarence (called Knox) and Lucille, also lived in the Bottom. They had three children—Sherman, Norman, and Clarence Jr. (called Bo Gator). Butch Carter, the son of Norman and his wife, Alma, was my age. The Scott family—Wilfred (called Scotty) and Blanche—lived in the Bottom before moving to Albany. They had three children—Barbara (who was about my brother German's age), Wilfred Jr. (who was about my brother Cliff's age), and Billy (who was my age).

North Side of Coeymans Creek Bridge

Some of the people live in other housing. Clarence and Cady Moore live about a mile north of the Hill in a small house along Route 144. The Moores have two children, Clarence Jr. (also known as Gandy and Chee Chee) and Mary (also known as Pooh Pooh). Gandy is my sister Sally's age, and Pooh Pooh is my sister Pearl's age.

John and Susie Moten live on the east side of Route 144 opposite the Bottom in a small house that they own. The house has small rooms and uneven floors, inside drinking water, electricity, and an outhouse. The Motens are the oldest Negro family in Coeymans. Susie is a founding member of Riverview Missionary Baptist Church and is regarded as the *mother* of the church. They have several children—Vet (Sylvester), Matt, Catherine, Sandra, Peonie, and Suzie. Peonie married Venable Jones and now lives in Selkirk. Two of her children, Mildred and Mary, are school classmates with my sisters Mary Lee and Pearl. Vet lives with his parents. He served in the army in his youth and refers to nearly everyone as "sir." He works as a service station attendant at Monk's garage in Coeymans. Sandra lives in Haverstraw, New York. She has a son named Charles, who is my age. We play together whenever he visits his grandparents.

Leonard "Len" Comithier and his wife, Lucinda (daughter of John Henry and Bernice Brewer), live in the apartment upstairs over Adamo's bar. They have several children—Delores (Bootsie), Leonard Jr., Eugene (Mickey), Betty, Perry, Arlene, Shelley, and Lisa.

Next door to Adamo's bar is an apartment building also owned by Joe Adamo. James and Gussie Bolden live on the second floor with their children, Richard Greene (Gussie's son), James Jr. and Larry. George Henry Lipscomb (the son of George and Lou Fanny) and his wife, Joan Hughes (the daughter of Mr. Teevy and Miss Jenny), live on the first floor.

Just before the Coeymans Creek Bridge and on the other side of the road lives John Henry Thomas Brewer and his wife, Bernice. The Brewers are prominent in the church. They have several children (John, Willie, Lucinda, Inez, Alphonso, Pearl, Clifford, Lawrence, Eleanor, Sheila, and Earl). Mr. Brewer serves as a deacon. He can often be heard in church as part of the *bark and call* between the pastor and the deacons. Many of his children are members of the choirs. Lucinda plays the piano. Inez is my Sunday school teacher.

The Brewers own their home as well as several acres of land around the house. Mr. Brewer is known around town as a fun-loving man. He always seems to have a smile and often a joke or two (or three). I heard him telling a few men about an old man. He said, "An old man told his drinking buddies that he bought an extra-long nightgown for his wife. The buddies asked him why he bought such a gown. The old man said that he has gotten so old that he thought that he would have more fun looking for it than he would after finding it." Everyone laughed loudly. Mr. Brewer has several nicknames that have since gotten abbreviated. Henry Thomas was shortened to Hen Tom, and Smack Me Down was shortened to Smack.

Mr. Brewer's oldest daughter, Willie, and her husband, Benny Deyo, live at the end of the Coeymans Creek Bridge next door to Willie Lee and Wildy O. Pounds. I have rarely seen Benny, a tall, rotund, and quiet man, without a cigar in his mouth.

The Brickyard

The Hudson River provides a natural highway for shipping and is used by many companies along its banks to ship products, particularly brick companies. Most of the Negro men in Coeymans work for the Powell & Minnock, Sutton & Suderly, and Roah Hook brick companies. As noted earlier, the Negro workers come from the Southern states of Virginia, North Carolina, and South Carolina and provide a pool of unskilled labor. The brick companies along the Hudson manufacture bricks from clay extracted from the hills along the Hudson. The clay is bulldozed and brought down the hill on trams, mixed with red paint, and placed into molds called brickbats. The brickbats are then fired in kilns. The bricks are removed from the kiln and loaded onto ships to be shipped down the Hudson River to suppliers around the country. The various work shifts are accentuated by the blowing of a loud whistle that can be heard throughout the Negro community and beyond. The first whistle is at seven in the morning, the second whistle at noon, and the third at three thirty. Most people set their clocks by the whistles.

My father's job is to take the bricks out of the kilns in order to free up the molds for new clay. As such, he goes to work at three thirty in the morning to get the bricks out as soon as they are cool enough to handle. My father is one of the more senior people working on the brickyard, and he prides himself with being one of the first at work. This gives him a slight head start on his work. It also gives him the rest of the day to work in his garden, slop the hogs, and chop wood. He finishes by ten thirty on a good day. Sometimes he has to work until noon if the bricks are not ready to be unloaded. Uncle Green, on the other hand, has the job of filling the molds and placing them in the kilns. He goes to work by seven in the morning and gets off work at three thirty in the afternoon.

The job does not pay much. My father takes home less than forty-five dollars a week. The company also takes out nine dollars every month for rent. In the wintertime from about Thanksgiving until mid-March, the Hudson River is frozen, and there is no work. All the workers draw unemployment benefits during these months. The unemployment benefits are less than his weekly pay. It is imperative to plant a garden in the summer, can as much food as possible, and raise pigs and chickens to help make ends meet.

Joe Palmer is an all-around handyman for the Sutton & Suderly Brick Company, and he is usually sent to handle any problems such as repairing steps or screen doors. When we finally got a refrigerator—a Philco—we did not have an electrical outlet to plug it up. At first, it was in the middle of the floor and plugged into the ceiling. Later, we got an extension cord and moved it to one side. Joe was around one day and saw that we had the refrigerator plugged into an extension cord. He volunteered to run an outlet from the ceiling to the wall near the refrigerator. He asked my mother not to tell anyone because if she did, he would get into trouble with his boss. He nailed the electrical line across the ceiling to the wall and down the side of the wall to about midway of the refrigerator. We were then able to plug in the refrigerator to a proper outlet.

Some of the men who worked on the brickyard lived in Albany and would drive down to Coeymans for work. Among them were Henry Hughes, Howard Hughes, William Hughes (son of Howard), Joe Tune, Curtis Robinson, and Oscar Turner. The company also provided housing on the brickyard for some of the men. The men are young and old, some married but without their spouses and others never married or widowed.

Among the men living on the brickyard are Heavy Davis, Burly Chapel, Levi, Duck Lee, and Smally to name a few. Smally has a reputation for drinking. Some of the men euphemistically refer to buying a bottle of liquor at Adamo's as "getting Smally out of jail." Among the most notable of the men on the brickyard are Weldon "the Champ" Brandon (Pauline Mason's father and brother of Miss Jenny and Miss Adie) and Ulysses Trap. These two are an odd couple, to say the least. They live in the upstairs of an old barn on the brickyard. They seem to get along well with each other until the weekends when one or the other or both get drunk. Invariably, they get into an argument. Usually, Trap accuses the Champ of doing something that Trap didn't like. The Champ, of course, denies it. Trap continues to gripe about it until the Champ hits him. Trap, being a rather frail man, ends up hurt for several days. He then complains that he cannot work because the Champ hit him.

There are times when neither of the men has been correct in his accusations. Trap would purchase cakes, cookies, and pastries and leave them out on the table. If he purchased them while he was drunk, he would forget that he had bought them. Some of us would help ourselves to these sweets. However, sometimes Trap did not forget about his purchases. When he did remember, he would accuse the Champ of eating up his food. The rest of the story remains pretty much the same with pretty much the same outcome too. The Champ knocks Trap around until he is too injured to go to work.

The Frangellas

The Frangella Mushroom Company is second only to the brickyard in employing Negroes. They have mushroom growing houses along the west side of Coeymans Creek next to the church and along the Hudson River across the street from the church parsonage. It is owned by members of the Frangella family and run by the brothers, Nick, Jimmy, Sandy, Carmine, and Johnny, and Nick's son Joe.

Similar to the brickyard, some of the workers at the mushroom plant are men from Virginia and the Carolinas. They, too, live in company housing of a sort. This housing is more like a western bunkhouse for men only. While these men are patrons of Mayone's grocery store and Adamo's bar, they do not usually attend Riverview Church. For the most part, they are men with limited education and no local family ties. They are paid minimum wages and rely upon Mayone's and Adamo's for credit in the same manner as the brickyard workers.

There is one worker who will be long remembered by all who come into contact with him. His name is Stanfield Turner, but everyone calls him Rat because of his facial features. Rat speaks in a manner that is difficult to understand, and only a few people do understand him when he speaks. He buys food items at Mayone's and eat them at Joe Adamo's. Yes, he does eat somewhat like a rodent. He is known to cook in the bunkhouse from time to time. One of the men reported that one time when he told Rat that a fly had fallen into his cooking pot, Rat responded, "Dat's meat right own!"

The work at the mushroom plant consisted mainly of picking mushrooms. The mushrooms are spawned in beds heavily fertilized with horse manure. The growing rooms are kept in darkness to enhance growing. The men wear battery-lit lights on their heads in order to see what they are picking in the growing rooms. The smell from the plant is obnoxious and tends to waft over most of the area of the Bottom and the Hill. In the warm summer months, the brickyard company housing on the other side of the creek will be covered with flies that tend to live off the horse manure at the mushroom plant. The otherwise yellow fly paper on the porches outside the houses will be virtually black with flies and fly excrement from the mushroom plant. The screens on the doors and windows are ineffective in keeping the flies out of the houses.

Other Negroes in town, young and old alike, also work for the Frangellas in various capacities in their homes and at the mushroom plant. Mrs. Eva Leigh, Tony Kittle's grandmother, does housekeeping work for Nick Frangella's wife, Frances. Corrine is a general maintenance man for some of the Frangellas. He does a lot of odd jobs around their homes, and they often feed him his meals. George Henry is becoming a right-hand man for Joe Frangella, the son of Nick Frangella. He works in a number of capacities and is often seen driving delivery trucks for the company. My brothers and sisters also work for many members of the Frangella family. Sally does housekeeping work for Nick's daughter, Patricia. Sally also works in a similar capacity for Johnny's wife, Helkie, and Jimmy's wife, Rose. Mary Lee works in a similar capacity for Julia, a sister of the Frangella brothers and the wife of Andrew Mayone. Pearl works in a similar capacity for Mary Orsini another sister of the Frangella brothers. Mary sometimes gives Pearl her old clothes as part of the payment for work. German works for Nancy Frangella, the wife of Sandy and the daughter of Joe and Marie Adamo. Clifford also works for Nancy. German, Clifford, and Eugene also work at the mushroom plant off and on. I work as a houseboy for Julia, Nancy, and Nancy's mother, Marie Adamo. My job is to polish furniture, clean windows, and wash floors. Sometimes I also cut the lawn and pull weeds from their gardens.

Adamo's Bar

Adamo's is a bar where the men gather to drink and play cards after work and on weekends. Some of the men go directly from work to the bar and stay until late at night. Since few of the families have bank accounts, Joe Adamo cashes their paycheck every Friday. This usually involves celebratory drinks of liquor or bottles of beer. My brothers and

I sometimes go to Adamo's for some of the men to get beer. Joe uses a half sheet of newspaper to wrap up the beer because he isn't supposed to sell it to minors. Our compensation is the return of empty beer bottles, for which we receive five cents apiece. The most popular beer is Dobler Ale followed by Ballantine and then Schaefer. Some men drink Genesee or Utica Club, but not too often.

The special drink for the men is the boiler maker—one shot of whiskey of any kind and a small bottle of beer. Although the beer is refrigerated, Joe never serves ice with liquor. The men drink liquors such as Bellows, Old Crow, and Rock N' Rye straight up or with a bottle of beer. Joe serves the drinks at the card table where the men seem to never leave. The men drink mostly beer during the week and liquor on the weekend after Joe cashes their paychecks. Some of the Negro women in town prepare dinners for the single men on Fridays who want to treat themselves to a good home-cooked meal after getting paid.

The card games can go on for quite a while, especially on weekends when Joe stays open later than during the week. Mr. Ben is regarded as one of the better players. My father plays from time to time, but I don't think he plays very well. He never seems to mention having won anything. Nor does he celebrate like many of the other men. Mr. William, a tall, slender man who looks much older than his years, also plays and often goes to sleep while playing. He lives on the Hill up the line from our house and is often seen going home. We wonder sometimes whether he will ever get home since he walks very slowly and seems to cross his steps in such a manner that it looks like he takes two steps backward for every step he takes forward. Somehow he eventually makes it home and is at work on the brickyard the next day.

My brothers German, Cliff, Gene, and I all have turns at cleaning up the bar after it closes. Sometimes we clean up the next day before Joe opens for business. Our job is primarily to sweep the wooden floor and keep it oiled. Joe pays us fifty cents for sweeping the floor and seventy-five cents if we have to also oil the floor. When we oil the floor, we use sawdust to absorb the excess oil, and it takes a bit longer to do the whole floor.

Mayone's Grocery

Andrew Mayone owns the local grocery store in the Negro community. The Negro women buy on credit during the week and pay Mr. Mayone at the end of the week. Unfortunately, during the winter months when the men are unemployed, some families can't afford to pay their bills off every week. My mother pays five dollars on her account and then asks for five dollars of "leftover meat." The leftover meat is that which has a bad smell or a little mold but is deemed salvageable. It is usually chicken parts and end cuts of meats. Mr. Mayone puts all this in a box and sends it home with my brother John, who works at the store.

Many in my family work for the Mayones. Mary Lee works for Andrew's wife, Julia, as a maid. Julia calls her Bell. John works for Andrew in the back of the store after he quit high school and before he went to work at West Point. Cliff, Eugene, and I work for Andrew at various times doing yard work at his new home on Frangella Avenue.

Riverview Missionary Baptist Church

According to the history of the church, Riverview Missionary Baptist church has its origins in 1924 when a small group of Negroes met for prayer in a shanty donated to them by the Sutton & Suderly Brick Company. The next year the people purchased some land and formed a mission under the name of Mount Sinai Church of Coeymans.

The church was built by Negro men with bricks donated by Sutton & Suderly and the Powell & Minnock brick companies. Three sisters of the church—Susie Moten, Rye Goodwyne, and Anna Coleman—gave the first three dollars to pay for the construction. Upon completion the church was renamed Riverview Missionary Baptist Church in August 1926. John W. Stroud was elected the pastor of the church. He was succeeded by three pastors before the Reverend N. G. Staggers became the pastor of the church in August 1931. Reverend Stagers remained pastor until June 1946 and was succeeded by Rev. Samuel B. Sutton in 1947.

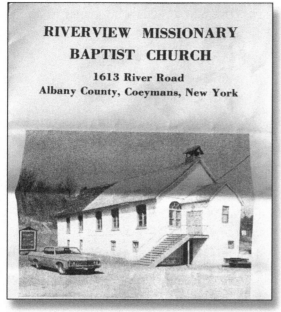

RIVERVIEW MISSIONARY BAPTIST CHURCH

1613 River Road
Albany County, Coeymans, New York

Riverview Missionary Baptist Church

The church is a gathering place for Negroes in Coeymans. The church building is situated on the west side of Coeymans Creek next to the entrance to the Frangella mushroom plant. The building itself is a two-story gray-and-white structure with a steep wooden staircase that leads to the sanctuary and a door underneath the staircase that leads to the kitchen, the Sunday school area, and bathrooms. The base of the building is cement block and brick, and the top is wooden with wood shingles. There are stained glass windows on the two sides of the church that were donated by various members of the church. On sunny days, the glow from the windows brightens the sanctuary. The names of the member who donated the windows are at the bottom of each one. At the back of the building is land that is used as our softball field now, but it can also be used for future expansion.

Reverend Sutton came from Buffalo, New York. His wife's name is Della, and they have three children—Helen Stevens (the wife of David Stevens and daughter of Reverend Sutton by his first wife), Pauline, and Bobby Felton (a foster child). Reverend Sutton's sermons are always laden with emotion and usually result in several of the women shouting uncontrollably after having been "touched by the Holy Spirit."

The church fellowships with other churches from Albany. Among the visiting churches are Morning Star Baptist Church and Macedonia Baptist Church. Visiting churches bring their choirs to sing and ministers to preach. On special days, such as the pastor's anniversary, several churches come to help celebrate and honor the pastor. This is usually an all-day affair at the church, including dinner. The ladies of the church spend most of Saturday preparing the meal to be served on Sunday. Sometimes they charge for the meal to raise funds for particular ministry activity at the church.

Joseph Fleming used to pick up children every Sunday and bring them to Sunday school. He would make several runs in different directions to get everyone to Sunday school. Mr. Fleming became ill like Miss Adie and passed away at an early age. Deacon Leonard Comithier took his place at picking up children for Sunday school. He is a kind and gentle man with an easygoing demeanor. I have never heard him say an angry word to anyone or about anyone. He gets along well with all the members of the church. He sets a great example for people young and old. His mother, a blind woman, lives in Catskill, a small village about thirty miles south of Coeymans. He often brings her to church as well. I do not know why, but he sometimes gets very ill and has to go to the hospital.

Everyone dresses up for Sunday school and church. It is also expected that you will bring your offering to Sunday school. Since I do not have twenty-five cents every Sunday, there are quite a few Sundays when I do not go to Sunday school or church. My Sunday school teacher, Mrs. Inez Stevens, said that I didn't have to bring money, but since everybody else seems to bring money, I don't want to be the only one not to bring an offering. All my friends in Sunday school and Mrs. Stevens know why I do not attend.

MY FATHER

There he sat in the kitchen in his work clothes, covered with red brick dirt from the brickyard, waiting for the bath water to heat on the woodstove. Underneath the dirt was a man about five feet eight inches tall, big feet (size 11 shoes), and hands laden with calluses from handing the bricks and farm tools. His hair without the brick dust is gray, and his head is near balding. He looked his age and more as lines appear to deepen in his forehead and cheeks, reflecting years of hard manual labor. He lifted his hand to take a puff off his ever-present Chesterfield cigarette and then relaxed it to his side, flicking the ash to the floor.

A big number-two tub sat in the middle of the floor where he would pour the hot water and then add some cold water to cool it off. My father's job is to remove the bricks that baked overnight from the dryer and stack them on pallets for shipping. He tries to get to work as early as possible so he can finish early in the day. He will then have time to fish or hunt or work in his garden before going down to Adamo's grill to drink and play cards.

It seems my father was always an old man. I never knew him to be a young man, although he must have been at some point in time. Not for me though. He was thirty-six when he married my mother and forty-eight when I was born. Sitting there, older than fifty now, he looks like an old man. I remember what he said when we asked if he had gone school. "I stopped school in the grade that I started in," he said with a smile. He was proud of the fact that he could yet read and write. He had lived a long, hard life before I was born. Now he has eleven living children (three having died at early ages) to feed and clothe.

"James Louis," came Mama's voice from the other room. "Get out of the kitchen and let your daddy take his bath."

"Gw'own, boy," said my father as he gazed up at me as if to say, "Mind your mama."

"I ain't stayin in here," I exclaimed to no one in particular, and in the same motion, I moved quickly out the back door to the porch.

Eric Lipscomb circa 1935

My father was born near Halifax, Virginia, on January 24, 1899, the second of ten children born to William Thomas Lipscomb (1872) and Sallie Carter (1875). Thom (as William was called) was the son of Moses Lipscomb (1830) and Minerva (1835). Sallie was the daughter of Mahala Moore (1834) and Isaac Carter (1838). Mahala's mother's name was Mary Moore, and Isaac's mother's name was

Edith. Thom and Sallie had ten children—Algie, Eric, Mary, Guy, German, Louis, Lloyd, Thom Jr., Cornelia, and Benny.

My father traveled around quite a few places as a single man, working here and there at various odd jobs before ultimately coming to Coeymans with John Henry Thomas Brewer in the 1920s. He worked for Allegheny Steel in Watervliet, New York, before taking a job on the Sutton & Suderly brickyard. Raymond Harris, a friend with a car, used to drive my father and other men to work at the steel plant. One day my father received a letter from the Suderlys stating that he could not stay in company housing unless he worked for the brickyard. My father quit his job at the steel company to work on the brickyard for less money in order to have a place to live.

My father was in Coeymans when my mother arrived in 1933. Although my mother lived in Dryfork, Virginia, less than ten miles from Tuberville, Virginia, where my father was raised as a child, they had not met before her arrival in Coeymans. With limited transportation available at the time, it was not unusual for people not to know neighbors who would be regarded as close by today. My mother and father were married in 1934 a little more than a year after her arrival in Coeymans.

We lived in the Bottom in the flat that Miss Nellie Mae Turner lives in now. After the Petersen's moved from the fourth house on the Hill (though there are no house numbers), we moved to that location. It seems that everyone has a large family, including us. In addition to Thomas Eric, Rosa Mae and Lois, all of whom died at an early age, there is (in order of age) Sally Ann, John Henry, German Ray, Mary Lee, Pearl Ann, Clifford Nathaniel, Eugene, James Louis, Janet Patricia, Carol Linda, and Deborah Jean.

The Dump

We can see him in the distance as he comes up the Hill toward the house. He always walked with a slight tilt to one side but sturdy. He has two gunny sacks—one in each hand. "Mama, Daddy comin'," somebody said. "Daddy, what you got?" said another. Daddy started to smile. I could see his teeth. "What you got, Daddy?"

"Daddy ain't saying nothin', but he got somethin!" Pearl exclaimed.

We now have him surrounded as if to help carry the bags, but nobody dares to touch the bags. Daddy doesn't want any help when he is about to bring home something good. "Daddy, you been to the dump?" Pearl asked.

"I stopped by for a while," he answered slowly with a smile and stepped through the doorway at the house. Mama looked at him, and he looked at Mama as if to get approval.

Mama said, "Where you been Lake? Over at that dump again? Don't be bringing that mess in here for these children to eat."

"You ain't got to eat it if you don't want to," he responded. "I was picking up some bread to feed the hogs when a Freihofer's truck drove up and started dumping out leftover stuff from Mayone's. I grabbed the boxes of stuff no sooner than de hit the ground. I ain't goin' to slop no hogs with it."

Mama wasn't so sure about the bakery truck story, but she cut her eyes back at us and said, "Y'all ain't got no business with no sweets this time of day. I'll put it up in the bread box for after yo dinna."

Daddy was staring at the table as if to say, "Don't I get a thank-you?" But he knew he just won, and that was good enough. This was not the first time he visited the dump and brought home something to eat. Nor would it be the last.

The Banjo

Although he cannot read music, my father plays both the guitar and the banjo. The guitar seems to be more of a challenge for him, and he doesn't play it often. He likes to play "The Deal," a tune about playing cards. He uses the back of his knife to slide up and down the strings. Corrine is a bit better at playing that song. However, you need to have patience with Corrine.

"You see, Uncle, it takes two turns on this string," Corrine begins to explain. "When you turn, you must stroke the strings to test the sound. If the sound ain't right, you turn the string again. But wait. Don't forget to turn the other strings a couple times. Now hold the knife against the strings for a touch. Then let go," he continues.

"Is it ready yet?" someone prods.

"Now, Uncle, you can't just play," he responds in a soft voice, unperturbed by the prodding and in no hurry. He turns a few more strings and places his hand on the guitar to strike a chord. One chord is all that he struck before he starts to explain further. "Uncle, 'The Deal' is an old tune. Yo daddy knows what I am talking about. Ask him."

"Could you play a little for us so we can get the hang of it?" one of the young men ask out loud.

"Well, Uncle, I don't play much anymore," he teases. "I'll have to see if my fingers can still do it. My arthritis keeps my fingers a little stiff nowadays," he explains, knowing full well he just played the song a few days ago as he has for as long as anyone can remember. This goes on for at least a half hour, and many think it's part of the warm-up for the song itself, which is only three minutes long—that is, if it's played without stopping. However, once he gets going, he brings tears and joy at the same time. The screech of the guitar is transformed into a melodic blues. He employs a *bark-and-response* technique that seems to go to your soul. Now everybody wants him to do it again. "Uncle, I am a little thirsty right now. I could use a big shot of Bellows and a small bottle of beer," he says with a soft voice in search of his reward.

Corrine plays the guitar, but nobody plays the banjo like my father. He loves the banjo, and it is his most prized possession. He doesn't play very often. Yes, he does tune the banjo from time to time, but he doesn't play until around the Thanksgiving and Christmas holidays. People from around town gather in our house to hear him play and taste some of his potato wine. Before long, after the spirits kick in, everyone is up dancing and laughing.

"River Joe," calls out James Mason, who had stopped by the house with Charlie Logan to bring Christmas greetings and get some of my father's wine. "Where's it at, man? I got some brick dust to wash down."

Daddy looks up at him with a straight face and says, "Lay down ass. Neither one of you hit a lick of work all week on the yard," he says, joking.

James continues, "River Joe, I know you got plenty around here. You goin' to make me ask twice on Christmas?"

"I don't care if you asked on Christmas or New Years," Daddy barks back. "I got a little put away in the other room."

"Well, all right then," said Charlie. "I knowed you had some. I can smell it."

"You can't smell your own shit. How can you say you smell my wine?" Daddy shoots back. "Vinie, get some glasses. I'm goin' to giv'em a little taste."

"River Joe, you're all right," they say almost in unison as they pull up a chair to the table.

The wine has been in the making since late September. Daddy makes potato wine in an oak barrel and keeps it near the woodstove in the kitchen. I am not sure how he made it. I do know that it contained raw white potatoes, raisins, yeast, and fresh water. The wine mixture is left to ferment for several weeks. Around the holidays it is ready to taste. The barrel has a spigot on it from which the wine is poured into Mason canning jars. As children, we sometimes *taste* the raisin residue in the barrel and find ourselves feeling *really good* and then really sick. Mr. Mason and Mr. Logan were the first to arrive as usual. Every year it

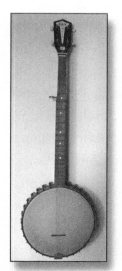

seems they say the same thing before getting a chair and a glass and staying for an indeterminate period. Others come and go, but Mr. Mason and Mr. Logan seem to stay as long as there is some wine in the barrel.

As the wine settles among the gathering, the banjo rings out with "Black Annie," my father's favorite song and about the only one he ever plays.

Kay shot his gun, Black Annie broke and run;
Cool drink of water, cool drink rye before I die.

The Banjo

37

> [doom doom doom, doom doom doom, doom doom doom doom
> doom doom doom]
> Don't care what my baby do, I love her just the same;
> Wear that red dress above her knees, I know she ain't playin.
> [doom doom doom, doom doom doom, doom doom doom doom
> doom doom doom]
> Oh by and by, Oh by and by, Oh by and by.

The words never seem to quite fit, but everyone seems to know what he means. This is a love song. Daddy repeats the lyrics over and over as he continues with riffs on the banjo and the gathering dances. "Lake, can't you play some Black Bottom music," says Mama as she strides across the floor with a slight twist of the hips.

The Trunk

The Trunk

My father did not have a bank account or a safety deposit box. However, he did have an old black army and navy trunk that he kept locked in his bedroom. No one was allowed to go into the trunk, and he did not open it with anyone in the room. We didn't know about all the things that he kept in the trunk, but we did know that he kept a pistol, some of his clothes, old bills, pictures, a money belt, and cash in the trunk. From time to time, he would take the pistol out to look at it. I never saw him use it, and I don't know what happened to it when he no longer had it. Although he did not make much money, on occasions like Christmas and when he wanted to go to Virginia, he would go to the trunk to retrieve some cash. It was not uncommon for him to go *home* to Virginia with his vacation money while we stayed home.

A Quiet Man

My father loved to fish and would always seem to find time to fish. Because he fished so often, my mother and many of his friends referred to him as Lake. He also fished in the Hudson and was nicknamed River Joe. Yes, it was polluted, but this was a time when America was not environmentally conscious. Among other fish, he caught bullheads (known in the South as catfish) and eels. His catches made the difference on the dinner table on many occasions.

My father was a physically strong man. The work on the brickyard required physical strength. He also needed the strength for gardening and chopping wood. Gardening was both a joy and a necessity for my father. He knew from childhood that plowing and planting fields put food on the table when money was scarce. Of course, the taste of potato wine was a by-product of the potato harvest. When the fall approached, my father would cut down tens of trees to provide firewood for the winter. The wood was later brought to the house by truck and cut up into small logs for use in the woodstove. We have a woodshed in back of the house to store the wood. We also stacked our back porch with wood for easy access during the night.

My father loved eggs, and he loved chicken. He would eat eggs (usually about a half dozen) several times a week. If we, the children, got eggs to eat, it was usually on a weekend. They were often scrambled and infused with baking powder, which caused the eggs to expand. My father's eggs were always cooked sunny side up with runny yolks. My father also got to eat the fried chicken before the children, or the best pieces were set aside for him. Ironically, I never heard my father ask for any particular food. I believe my mother wanted to acknowledge my father as the breadwinner of the family.

Although we played together as children, we never played outside or inside with my father. We did not ask him to play or to take us anywhere, and he rarely did. I guess he was just too old and too busy to play. He would yell at us sometimes, but he did not whip us. My mother did all the reprimanding. Most of time when he was not working at the brickyard, working in the garden, cutting wood for the stoves in the house, or drinking down at Adamo's, he could be found sitting inside or outside the house with a Chesterfield cigarette and a bottle of Dobler beer. Sometimes I would hear him talking to himself. None of it was ever very clear, but it was a conversation of some length. He was mostly a quiet man when it came to his children.

My father also seemed to have quiet relationships with my two uncles who lived in Coeymans. My uncle McKinley would often visit with Mr. Paul, who lived next door to us, but he rarely came to our house. My father would visit Aunt Mary, his sister, in the Bottom, but usually when Uncle McKinley was not there. My uncle Green would come downstairs to talk to my mother, but rarely did he have a long conversation with my father. I never saw my father go upstairs to visit Uncle Green. Yet all three men were quite conversant with other people in Coeymans. I am sure there is a story behind their relationship, but it has not been shared with me.

Although he did not attend church, my father believed in the *Master* and that all things in life are in accordance with God's plan. He often remarked that the people in the church *worried* God too much. He would say from time to time, "The people worry the Lord so much that if He had anything to give them, He wouldn't give it to them." To his friends, he was an honest man with a strong character. However, he was not without a joke, prank, or smile in dealing with them. Young men, like Joe Tune, Jimmy Boxley, and Oscar Turner, seemed to gravitate to him because he was willing to share the gifts of practical wisdom and knowledge that he had gained over the years.

MY MOTHER

"Mama, you all right?" I asked.

"I am okay. I just need to take my medicine," she replied. Mama, a fair-skinned Negro woman with black hair (it was never gray), was sitting at the kitchen window with an ointment-laden cloth tied on her head and a needle and thread in her hands. The sun, pouring through the window, created a photographic opportunity that was not to occur. She was working on a quilt from some cloth Mary Lee, my sister, had given her.

"Why don't you take your medicine?" I asked.

"I don't have the money for the prescription. I have to wait until Lake gets paid, and I'll buy a few pills then. Medicine is high, and we can't afford to buy too much." Mama had a brown paper bag with several kinds of pills for various health problems that now plagued her life. None of the pills were for the latest prescription. "Y'all gone outside and play. I'll be all right." This is the mother I remember.

Vinel Lee Motley was born in Dryfork, Virginia, on April 30, 1913. Her mother, Annie Lipford (1879), died when she was three years old. Annie was the daughter of Harrison Lipford (1841) and Beckie (1850). Annie was the fifth wife of Joseph Motley (1859), and my mother was the youngest of her eighteen children. Joe had been born a slave by Liza Fitzgerald, a slave woman and her slave master. It was said that Joe had a total of forty children by four of his five consecutive wives. One of his wives died at the altar after the wedding, and he subsequently married her sister.

Joseph Motley   Annie Lipford Motley

My mother was raised by her oldest half sister, Elizabeth, whom she called "Sis Lize." She was apparently named after her grandmother. Before coming to Coeymans, my mother lived with her father, Sis Lize, her brother Jacob, Jacob's wife (Veenie) and her sister Bertha. My mother was a strong-willed person who did not hesitate to let her feelings be known. She often talked about the time she swung an ax at her brother Jacob when he tried to reprimand her.

My mother came to Coeymans in 1933 and stayed with her brother Green Motley. Being a young fair-skinned woman, she caught the attention of the men in Coeymans, including Jim Breedlove and James Smith. However, she fell in love with my father, a man who at thirty six years old was almost twice her age.

After their wedding in 1934, my mother and father rented one of the company houses in the Bottom next door to Jenny Hughes, a young

Vinel Lee Motley circa 1936

woman my mother's age who became her best friend. The flat consisted of four rooms without electricity or plumbing. The company provided white paint to whitewash every room. It contained a strong odor that served as a disinfectant. My mother would paint all the rooms and wash the bare wood floors with disinfectant. The flat was heated by a woodstove and lit by kerosene lanterns.

The Fourth House on the Hill

The bottom flat of the fourth house on the Hill used to be occupied by Lilly and Howard Petersen before they moved to New York City. When they moved, my mother took the unusual step of going down to the office at the brickyard and asked whether her family could move into the flat next to her brother. With their permission, we moved to the fourth house on the Hill on the ground floor beneath Uncle Green and Aunt Francis, where we stayed until 1962. Our flat consisted of a kitchen, a dining room, a living room, three bedrooms, and a walk-in closet. The flat had no utilities. The kitchen had a woodstove, an icebox, and three water pails for drinking water. In time we got electricity, a gas stove, and a refrigerator, but we never did get indoor plumbing. The house was heated by a potbelly wood/coal stove in one of the large bedrooms. The pail—or slop jar, as our portable toilet was called—was in the hall near the door. It was actually a five-gallon can with a handle on it. We used the pail in lieu of going outside to the outhouse at night.

My parents had a bedroom, and the children slept in the remaining two bedrooms. At one point, John Henry (until he left home), Clifford,

Eugene, and I slept in one bed on one side of the room, and Pearl, Janet, Linda, and Deborah slept in the bed on the other side of the room. Sally and Mary Lee slept in the other bedroom that also served as a dining room sometimes, and German slept in a small area at the end of the hall. Everyone washed up in the kitchen, taking turns using the wash basin during the week and the tin tub on the weekends.

Our house had several insect and vermin problems. We could cope with the rats that came from the garbage dump in back of the woodshed by placing steel traps underneath our beds. Roach sprays kept the roaches under control or at least manageable. However, the spiders and the flies were difficult to deal with. The flies during the summer months were everywhere, notwithstanding the flypaper and the fly spray. In order to sleep, we would cover our face up with pieces of curtain to avoid swallowing flies. Invariable, if you swallowed a fly, within a half hour after you woke up, you would throw up. This was particularly nauseating and more so if you didn't have anything in your stomach to throw up. So it was with the spiders. If a spider bit you at night, it was usually on the lip. The next morning or sometime during the day, your lip would swell up so big that you could not close your mouth. It was particularly embarrassing to go to school with a fat lip. All the Negro kids knew that a spider had bitten you on the lip, but the white kids would always look in wonderment.

The flat was in poor condition. The floors consisted of uneven boards with knots where often you could see through to the ground, and we used tin can tops to seal up holes that were made by rats. The linoleum covered most of the floor but did not last very long because of its poor quality and the wear and tear of the people in the house. The walls were made of plaster over slats that had deteriorated over time. We used wallpaper to cover the holes and smooth out the look of the walls. The smoke from the woodstoves and the kerosene lamps yellowed the ceilings and the wallpaper. Nonetheless, my mother, who was pregnant most of the time, did virtually all the maintenance around the house. She whitewashed the ceilings (to disinfect them from fly excrement as well as to brighten them up), hung the wallpaper, and laid the linoleum.

For many years we did not have a washing machine. The family wash was done outside in a number-two tub. My mother would build a fire under the tub and wash the clothes on a washboard, wring them out by hand, and hang them on the clothesline. Later my father bought a handwringer that could be bolted to a table. We did not get an electric washing machine until the late 1950s. We never did get an automatic washer.

Although we were regular visitors to the doctors' office (or they were regular visitors to our house), my mother had several home remedies that she would use whenever any of the children got sick. We were given "Save the Baby" on a teaspoon of sugar for our colds. She used chopped onions in alcohol wrapped in a baby's diaper around our stomachs to break any fever. Sometimes ginseng weed was used on the forehead for the same purpose. A hot flannel with ointment was worn on the chest to cure colds.

Shopping for Her Children

Saturday was the day to go to the market. When she didn't go to Mayone's, my mother sometimes would go to Albany with Uncle Green and Aunt Frances to get grocery at the Albany Public Market and do some shopping. The groceries always cost more money than she had. She would buy in bulk as much as possible and often received leftover meat and chickens at a bargain price. Paul, the person in charge of meats at the market, would give her a Tobin Packing fifteen-by-forty-eight-inch box of meat and chicken for about five dollars. The items were usually somewhat spoiled but salvageable when she could remove the mold.

My mother would shop at Millham's, a clothing store near the grocery store in Albany. The clothes were cheap and did not last too long. The black pants would turn reddish when you washed them, and they smelled like a freshly plucked chicken. Charlie Millham, the owner, sometimes would load his car up and drive through Coeymans, selling his goods to the people on the Hill and in the Bottom, generally on credit. I remember the time Mr. Millham came to the house when we were killing the pigs (the Saturday after Thanksgiving). My uncle had just finished removing the pig intestines, and my mother was in the process of cleaning them in the house. The foul smell was overwhelming.

"Who's at the door?" Mama asked out loud but to no one in particular.

"It is Mr. Millham," Pearl responded. "He's standing outside near his car."

"Tell him come on in," my mother said.

Pearl ran out the door and stood in front of Mr. Millham and said, "She said for you to come on in."

Mr. Millham's face turned a bright red, and he rolled his eyes as if to scare Pearl. Then said, "I'd like her to come out to the car."

Pearl said, "She can't come right now. She is doing the chitlins."

Mr. Millham looked beside himself and said finally said, "I just got a few things for the children to try on. They can try them on out here to see if they fit."

Pearl turned and ran back to my mother and said, "He says that he don't need to come in and that he wants us to try on some clothes outside." Mama stopped cleaning the chitlins, wiped off her hands on her apron, and came to the screen door.

Mr. Millham walked over closer to the door and said, "Mrs. Lipscomb, how are you today? I just got a few things for the children to try on. We got some very nice prices."

Mama looked at him as if to see right through him and said in about as reserved a tone as I have ever heard her speak, "We don't want no clothes this week." Then she walked away from the door.

All Her Children

Children always seemed to be a part of my mother's life. She not only had fourteen children of her own, but she also often found herself surrounded by the children of the community. The children seemed to feel comfortable around her, and they could be found at our table along with my brothers and sisters. She would often share watermelon or some other treat with the children gathered at our house. As time passed, our house was filled with grandchildren, most of which lived with us for periods of time. My mother would take care of them as her own, including feeding, clothing, housing, and tending to medical needs. She loved children and always seemed to have a kind word for them. They in turn loved her and regarded her as if she were their mother.

Leroy, the son of my oldest sister, Sally, was the first grandchild. As a first grandson, he was given a lot of attention, and it seemed to some of us that he was favored over the rest of us. What we didn't realize was that with my mother, all children are favored. In time we came to appreciate that quality in her. Nonetheless, we did get a little revenge on the favored grandson.

As was typical of the summertime, Cliff, Gene, and I had picked some blackberries for my mother to make a blackberry cobbler. Leroy was used to getting first dibs on all food. On the Sunday the cobbler was made, Leroy took a nap in the afternoon that somehow extended into the early evening. My mother served dinner early as was the custom on Sundays, and we all had cobbler for dessert. My mother left some cobbler for Leroy. However, Cliff decided he wanted some more. He went into the kitchen and spooned all the berries out of the cobbler, leaving nothing but the juice and the crust. Leroy awoke and quickly ate his dinner in anticipation of his cobbler. When he discovered that his cobbler didn't have any berries in it, he began to wail loudly. My mother didn't know what was wrong with him. He tried to explain while crying at the same time, and the words came out garbled. "I ain't got nothin' but da juice!" We looked at him, grinning from ear to ear without my mother seeing us. The more we grinned, the more he cried and pointed at us. My mother was confused as to why he would accuse us of something when it was clear that we had not done anything to him (or so it seemed). He cried and moaned for the rest of the day and well into the night.

Mama's Health

My mother seemed to be in bad health for as long as I knew her. I am sure it was not only hereditary but also the result of hard work and giving birth to fourteen children. She suffered from epilepsy, and we often found ourselves having to put a spoon wrapped in cloth in her mouth to avoid her biting her tongue and grinding her teeth. The seizures could happen at any time, but they were usually a result of her high blood pressure. Dr. John Mosher and Dr. Ira Lefevre, the local doctors, would make regular house calls. My mother would visit the doctor's office when she was well enough to walk over there. She had a variety of prescriptions for her nerves, high blood pressure, heart, and diabetes. She would not stop working even when the doctor told her to rest.

"Jame Louis, come heah. Yo mama having a fit again."

"Daddy, I'm comin' with the spoon. I have to get a cloth to wrap it in." Mama was having an epilepsy seizure. "Okay, I got the spoon. Can you get her mouth open?" My father pried open Mama's mouth, and I put the spoon in so her teeth could rest on the handle. It seemed as if every muscle in her body was being twisted as she lay on the bed unconscious. "Should we call Dr. Mosher? Take her to the hospital?" I asked no one in particular.

My father said, "No, she be all right after a while. Get a wet towel so we can put it on her head," he said. Somebody ran to get the towel. By this time, the bed was surrounded with children waiting to see what would happen next. We put the towel on her head and watched. It may have been a short while, but it seemed like forever before Mama opened her eyes and turned her head to see everyone staring down upon her. "Vinie, you want to go to the hospital?" my father asked.

"No, I am not going to no hospital. I'll be all right," she said. "Let me rest awhile. I got to fix suppa," she said.

"Mama, I can fix something to eat," said Mary Lee. Mama looked at Mary Lee as if to say, "That's my job!" It wasn't long before Mama was up and in the kitchen as if nothing had happened. Unfortunately, these *fits* happened with some frequency and at different times of day or night. I was always concerned that one day it would happen for the final time.

Zion Songs

My mother did not socialize much. Occasionally, she would visit a few friends such as Miss Sara, Miss Jenny, Aunt Mary, Aunt Francis, and Rosa Logan. From time to time, these ladies might stop by to see my mother, but it was mostly Aunt Frances, Aunt Mary, and Miss Sara. My mother stayed home most of the time. She did not attend church, although she believed in God and seemed to almost constantly be humming Zion songs from long ago. Too often, it seemed, she sat at home alone with the children. She would either be sewing (by hand) or rocking a child in the rocking chair. She often talked about being alone. She wished she had gotten to know her mother. In a moment of despair, she once said to me, "One of these days, my lips will be cold." I did not appreciate the comment until I kissed her lips many years later at her funeral. They were indeed cold. Her eulogy, in part, reads as follows:

> She loved her family. Her life was characterized more by giving than receiving. Her will and desire to make and see people happy was perhaps her greatest asset and contribution to those with whom she came in contact. Each family member was special to her. We will miss that special attention. Lord, give each of us that unique quality in which you let her specialize.

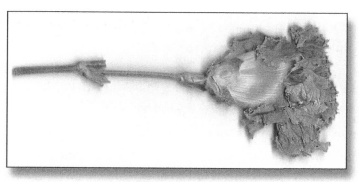

Vinel's Last Flower

MY AGE OF INNOCENCE
1952–57

Memory Lane—Recollections

There are some things that occurred in my early childhood that I will always remember.

The Vendors

There were a few vendors that were like family in that they regularly came by the house.

- ***Rag Man.*** Like a town clarion, the man moved through the Negro community on any weekday. "Rag-g-g-g, rag-g-g, rag-g-g." This was his way a letting you know that he was there to pick up anything made of cloth that you would like to discard. He would pay ten cents a pound for the cloth items. I never understood why he would come by so often given that most of the people barely had enough clothing to wear let alone to throw away.

- ***Insurance Man.*** The short, balding white man with the smile on his round face would lightly tap the door and immediately open the door and enter the house without waiting to be asked inside. "How are you, Mrs. Lipscomb?" he would ask. "I am doing fine," my mother would respond. "Do you care for any coffee? I got a pot on the stove." The man would invariably accept the offer and was soon sitting at the table. "Mrs. Lipscomb, I need a $1.90 this week for the policies. I skipped last week and need to catch up some on the payments." "I can give you a dollar this week and a dollar next week. Would that work?" my mother responded. "Well, it will help, but I've got to catch up here."

- ***Salesman.*** "Mama, that salesman is here," said one of the children. "Tell him I am not home," my mother said. The child turns to the salesman and said, "She said she is not home." The salesman had a distraught look on his face, but he backed away from the door slowly and then retreated to his station wagon vehicle filled with various household products.

- ***Milkman.*** Milk came in glass bottles. It was necessary to set the empty bottles out for the milkman, and he would leave an equal number of full bottles. "Mama, the milkman is at the door." "Tell him I don't have no money today," said Mama. "Tell your mother that I can't leave any milk unless she pays the bill," said the milkman. Mama came to the door to speak with the milkman. "I don't have no money today. I will pay you Friday when Lake gets his check. You don't have to leave any milk."

An Ax-cident

Some Saturdays my mother would go with my uncle Green to Albany to buy groceries at the Albany Public Market, and we would stay at home, playing. One of those Saturdays, I was playing with the wood that had been stacked up by the stove. Next to the wood was a small ax that we referred to as a hatchet. I kept chopping at the wood log with this hatchet that I could barely lift. After not too long, I missed the log and the ax landed on my foot. I was completely numbed by the pain. My mouth was locked into place, and I could not scream. As I pulled the ax away, the blood seemed to gush from my foot. I then let go of a loud scream and began to hop around. I believe it was John Henry who grabbed me and started to squeeze my foot to get the blood to stop. Around the same time, my mother was coming through the door. She quickly grabbed a piece of a sheet or diaper, put some salve on it, and wrapped my foot. My foot swelled up, so I couldn't put a shoe on. That night I had to sit up all night in a chair and keep the injured foot in warm water and witch hazel. I was not taken to a doctor. The next morning the swelling was gone, but the gash in my foot was open. My mother put a piece of white cloth on the wound and taped my foot tight with *inch* tape. The gash would heal, but I still carry the scar on my right foot today.

My Tricycle

There are times in your life when you feel that you have been wronged. I've had a few of those times, but I still remember the first time. I was about five years old, and I had a tricycle. Mickey Gladney, the sister of my friend Jimmy, who lived up the line from our house, was playing in our yard. She asked me if she could ride my bike, and I said no. She decided to ride the bike anyway and began to peddle away from me. I ran after her as she peddled over to my neighbor's yard. I caught up with her and pulled her off the bike. Just as I was pulling her off the bike,

Anne Lee Wilson, my neighbor, came out of her house. All she saw was this girl crying and me pulling her off the bike. She stopped me from taking my bike back and took me home. She told my mother that I was beating up Mickey. I didn't get a chance to explain anything. My mother gave me a whipping on the spot with the switch (a small supple branch from a tree). Ann Lee and Mickey got to watch! After that, I had to stay in the house for the rest of the day. I remained angry at Miss Wilson and Mickey for a very long time.

Nicodemus and Little Sim

My older sister Pearl would bring books home from school that she would sometime read to Eugene and me. My favorite books were about Nicodemus and Little Sim. I did not know or understand at the time that these books, written by Inez Hogan, would later be called "pickaninny" books. Much of the language in the books was colloquial to me, although the caricatures were exaggerated. Nonetheless, we wanted Pearl to read to us about Nicodemus and Little Sim.

Nicodemus had a gang—Clara Bell, Little Sim, Petunia, Obadiah, Rastus, and Little Sister. One of my favorite stories was about building a clubhouse. The gang wanted a clubhouse, but no one seemed to know how to build one. The gang got the clubhouse built except for the roof when they ran out of money. They ended up arguing over who would own the house. Eventually, the clubhouse got a canvas roof, and everyone contributed something to complete it.

It is difficult to criticize the book today given the cultural standards at the time of the writing. However, today they inform all of us of our past and how far we have come from the days of the books formerly prominently found in public school libraries.

George Reddy and Pa Frosty

George Reddy lived in the fifth house on the Hill before the Rays. From time to time, he would work around our house for a meal or two. In the wintertime it was not unusual to see him sit by our potbelly stove, and he never seemed to move. He was an elderly, balding man of about five feet seven inches tall with a grayish beard. When he died, it was said that his spirit was still in the house. Somehow, this was reinforced by an event that happened to our dog. The dog was barking one night in the hall. A sudden clap or slap was heard, and the dog became silent. The next day we noticed that the dog walked with his head to one side. Everyone said it was because the spirit of George Reddy had slapped the dog.

Alex "Pa Frosty" Bates was another elderly man who lived around town. He was a relative of Clarence Moore and used to work for Aaron Tinkle, a white man in Ravena until he got too old. It was not long before he became homeless, and he didn't seem to ever take a bath. He would wander around town and get handouts wherever he could. Sometimes he would go over to the town dump and scavenge food and clothing. In the winter he would come by our house and sit by the stove. My mother would not turn anyone away in the wintertime. He might wander over to someone else's house and do the same thing. At night he slept wherever he could, sometimes in our woodshed and at other times on the streets in Ravena. One day he was found in his eternal sleep on Main Street in Ravena.

Words that I Remember

Many of the Negroes in Coeymans did not have a formal education. Most of what they knew was learned through experience. Sometimes their speech came out somewhat phonetically because of their attempt to repeat what they thought they heard other people say. Also, there were slang expressions that were just part of the local discourse. It always seemed odd to me that the intent of the expressions were often just the opposite of what was being said.

- Mr. Paul would often use the phrase "Com'nissa" to indicate that an event had started. For example, he would say, "The chiren com'nissa running," meaning that the children had started to run.
- My mother would say that if you did something wrong, the "tight leg man was gonna take you to Judge Albano and make you smoke," meaning that the state trooper would take you before the justice of the peace.
- When the women at church agreed with something another person was saying, they would often respond, "Honey, hush," or they'd say, "You'd better shut your mouth."
- If you didn't "set horses" or became "unbenefit" with people, it meant that you did not get along well with them or that you had gotten into an argument with them.

Take Your Time, Son

I discovered at an early age that I could not speak as well as other children. No matter how hard I tried to say certain words, I could not get them to come out. When I was asked a question and found that I could not answer, I would try any way. It usually came out as stuttering. My uncle Green also stuttered. One day my mother sent me upstairs to ask my uncle for something. (I don't remember what.) When I tried to ask him, I was hopelessly stuttering. He looked at me and said, "Tttta-aa-a-kk-ee yo ... ttttt-immme sssson!" I wanted to laugh. Then I realized that he was a grown man with my problem, and he was trying to give me some advice. It turns out that his advice has been sage for me.

What Was Your Name?

It seemed that everyone was called by a name different than the one they are born with. Some of the nicknames are so commonplace that they took the place of your real name. For example, my father was rarely if ever called Eric other than by Dr. Mosher and Dr. Lefevre. Everyone called him Lake or River Joe. So it was with me.

As a baby, I had dimples, and my hair was braided. Our neighbor, Miss Dicey, thought I looked like a girl and started calling me Little Oughta Be, her shorthand for "ought to be a girl." To my knowledge, she and one of her daughters, Ann Lee, were the only two people who ever used that name.

As the baseball players in the Negro league became popular and began entering the major league, players like Jackie Robinson, Roy Campanella, and Don Newcombe became heroes and household names in the Negro community. Don Newcombe and I are both left-handed, and for that reason, older boys like my cousin Lenzy Motley started calling me Newcomb. Soon everyone called me Newcomb. Still quite young, I thought that was my name. When I started school in first grade, I learned my real name. However, by that time, I led two lives—Jimmy in school and Newcomb everywhere else. I continued with the two first names throughout my school years.

By the time I went to college, I was an admirer of a British actor named James Mason and the formality that seemed to accompany his name. I decided that I was going to be called by my formal name as well. It certainly would alleviate the usual head turning when people called me Jim or Jimmy and five heads turned at the same time. Few people used their formal names. I thought that once I became known as James, I would know when I heard the name "James", the party was more than likely speaking to me. The problem was with the people who hung up on me, thinking they had the wrong number when I answered the telephone as James.

Friends I Was Born With

I knew every Negro in Coeymans. They were all more or less friends if not relatives. I was always older or younger than my friends. People like Earl Brewer, Leonard Comithier, Mickey Comithier, Betty Comithier, Pamela (which we pronounced Palma) Wilson, Jeannie Leigh, and Delores Comithier were all older than me and friends of my brothers and sisters. Although other Negro boys, such as John Thunderbird, Billy Scott, Frankie Thurman, Butch Carter, Jimmy Hunt, and James Bolden, would come and go over time, Jimmy Gladney was the only Negro boy in town my age who remained over the time I lived in Coeymans. Jimmy lived up the line in the seventh house on the Hill. He was a fearless individual and seemed to be willing to try anything. I cannot forget the time I watched Jimmy kill a cat he believed to be sickly. First, he tried to drown it in Coeymans Creek, but the cat kept swimming to shore. Then he buried it alive. I was too shocked to tell anyone until now. I wasn't exactly as adventuresome, but I regarded him as one of my best friends. We did just about everything together except swim. I had not learned to swim, so I stayed away from the water.

Bobby and Tony Wilson lived next door with their mother, Louise, with their grandparents, Paul and Dicey Wilson. Bobby was older, and Tony was younger than me. They only lived in Coeymans a short time before they moved to Albany. We continued to see them when they visited their grandparents and sometimes when we went to Albany to get our haircut. They have remained lifelong friends.

Tony Kittle, Perry Comithier, and Billy Stevens were all younger than me by a year or two. These were my Monopoly buddies and probably the friends I got to know the best. We were like brothers. Tony and I often had talks about our personal life (such as it was at our age). One of my most difficult tasks was to meet Tony one day after school to tell him that his cousin Johnny Foy had died in the hospital. We had expected his death, but we really didn't quite understand what it would mean. I know he was comforted by the fact that I was there for him at that time. Billy was the only child in the family at the time. His father had been killed in Korea, and he was living with his mother, Virginia (Virgie), and his grandparents, Mitchell and Lena Stevens. I would go to his house often to play with the many toys that he received from his aunts and uncles. Billy seemed to have every new toy on the market. Billy was always willing to share with others. We would spend endless hours working on his erector sets or model battleships.

Penny Candy

Part of my age of innocence was my love for penny candy. It was a time when you could actually buy candy for a penny. My mother would send my older brothers and sisters to the store to buy twenty-five cents' worth of penny candy on Sunday afternoon. Pape's Confectionery had the best penny candy. Mrs. Pape, the proprietor was an elderly Italian lady well past retirement age. She lived on the premises. She could hardly walk around the store, and many times her daughter would come to assist her. She would carry Mary Janes, Hershey's Kisses, Juicy Fruits, Good & Plenty, licorice, and chocolate balls. Her competition was Cappolarello Grocery located next door. Mr. Cappolarello was also an elderly Italian man around the age of Mrs. Pape. He also lived on the premises with his wife. His candy tended to cost a little more, but you could get Sugar Daddys at his store. Both of these proprietors were dependent upon the patronage of the Negro community. Sometimes a few of the youth would shoplift from the store. In an effort to catch the youth involved, Mr. Cappolarello started asking certain youth to sign their names on a piece of paper. Little did the youth know that he intended to turn the names over to the police. Unfortunately, he asked some youth to sign their names even though they were not involved in the improper conduct. To Mr. Cappolarello, all the Negro youth looked alike. It was this incident that caused the youth to stop patronizing the store.

Bruno's was the other store in town that sold penny candy. This store was also run by an elderly Italian lady. Mrs. Bruno also carried all the newspapers and served as the local bus stop for Greyhound, Trailways, Shortline, and Mountain View bus lines. We would go to her store if we were going down to Chubby's Grocery on Westerlo Street since it was on the way. She had several sons, one of whom we called BI. I do not know how he got the nickname. He was known in the Negro community because he used to be the ragman that collected the rags. Later in life he also sponsored the Southwind softball team. This was an all-white team that had a rivalry with Three Star Barbershop, an all-Negro team from Albany. Many of the members of the Albany team grew up in Coeymans and still had relatives in Coeymans.

As we got older, we went to the store by ourselves. We carried back the soda bottles—Royal Crown, Coca Cola, Hires Root Beer, and Pepsi—to receive a two-cents deposit for each bottle. We used the money to buy penny candy. If we had enough money, we would buy "Lick'em Ades," a Kool Aid powder that children would eat dry. When I got my job working for the Motens, my penny candy supply was increased when Mrs. Moten gave me small bags of penny candy on Saturdays.

Riverview Missionary Baptist Church—The Choirs

The church was known for its wonderful choirs. The young men and women of the day would practice during the week. It was commonplace in the summer to sit outside the church and listen to the choirs rehearse. The Brewers, Wilsons, Lipscombs, Foys, and Comithiers all had beautiful voices. Some of the notables I remember include Joan Hughes, Alfonzo Brewer, Barbara "Jeanie" Leigh, Pearl Lipscomb, Clifford Lipscomb, Sammy Blanton, Leon Wilson, Pleasant Foy, and Alvin Foy.

Most of us used to listen to Brother Ivory on WABY radio on Sunday mornings before going to church. He would play the songs by artists such as Mahalia Jackson, Clara Ward, the Five Blind Boys, James Cleveland, the Soul Stirrers, the Dixie Humming Birds, and the Mighty Clouds of Joy. Songs by these artists were also sung by our choirs. I would love to hear Sammy Blanton and Leon Wilson vie for honors singing their versions of the songs we heard on the radio.

The choirs would prepare special songs for the pastor's anniversary. I never did go to church on the pastor's anniversary, but I did go over to the church during the week to hear the choirs rehearse. I never knew the name of my favorite song. I only knew a few of the words that I heard Alvin "Pop" Foy, a younger brother of Pleasant Foy, sing over and over, "I cried holy. I cried holy. I cried holy." It was years later that I learned that the song was actually a gospel hymn that goes by many variants such as, "I Fell on My Knees and Cried Holy," "I Bowed on My Knees," "I Cried," and "I Bowed Down on My Knees." The words of the various versions are similar, but the music seems to differ by ethnicity. Now that I have heard various versions, I am reasonably certain that Pop sung the words of Nettie Dudley Washington but that he also added his own emotion-laden gospel rendition.

I dreamed of that city called Glory, so bright and so fair,
When I entered the gate, I cried, "Holy." The angels all
    welcomed me there.
They led me from mansion to mansion, and, oh, the sights I saw.
But I said, "I want to see Jesus, the one who died for all."

Refrain
Then I fell on my knees and cried,
"Holy. [Holy.] Holy. [Holy.] Holy. [Holy.]"
I fell at His feet and sang, "Glory. [Glory.]
Glory to the Son of God. [Of God.]"

Pleasant Foy was perhaps the most versatile singer of them all. He would sing a variety of songs in his own style as well as that of others. Some of my favorites by him were a song made famous by Rev. James Cleveland called "Peace Be Still" and a song sang by Sam Cooke as a member of the gospel group The Soul Stirrers called "The Last Mile of the Way."

Young and old alike sang in the several choirs at the church. The choirs have seen different members over the years, but they always seemed to maintain a reputation of excellence in the Albany Capital District. Some of my favorite songs by the choirs were "Leaning on the Everlasting Arm," "This Is My Story," "I Need Thee," "At the Cross," "What a Friend We Have in Jesus," "Blessed Assurance," "God Will Take Care of You," "In the Garden," "Just a Closer Walk with Thee," "His Eye Was on the Sparrow," "I Said I Wasn't Gonna Tell Nobody," and of course, "I Got Shoes." These songs resonated well with the times for the Negro people in Coeymans. They provided everyone with the sense of God's presence and His deliverance regardless of our then circumstances.

Coeymans Elementary School

We attended school in Coeymans and Ravena that over time became the Ravena-Coeymans-Selkirk Central School District, a combination of schools for the region. The Coeymans School building, originally built by Acton Civill (1804–89) to house a polytechnic institute, was purchased in 1899 by the local board of education and was used for the elementary and junior high school until 1963.

Coeymans School

There was a World War I war memorial in front of the Coeymans School. I was always proud of the fact that I knew the one Negro person whose name was on the memorial—Brummy Watkins. He had been around Coeymans for a long time and served in the army. This was not only unusual for a town like Coeymans, but it was also unusual that a Negro man served in combat at all. I never asked Mr. Brummy whether he served in an integrated unit, but since the military was not integrated until World War II, he most likely served in a segregated unit. It was several years later that I learned that my father's oldest brother, Algie Lipscomb (who lived in North Carolina, a segregated state in the South), had also served in World War I in a segregated infantry unit.

I had many white friends at school, but our friendship for the most part began and ended with the school day or school event. There was little or no interaction or communication outside of the school environment. Negroes did not go outside of the Negro community other than to work, to shop at the stores, or to see a movie at Connery's Theatre in Ravena.

I remember my elementary school days by specific events. I did not go to kindergarten. I began school in the first grade, and Mrs. Childs was my teacher. Mrs. Childs was (or seemed to be) very much a senior citizen who spoke with a soft voice and walked slightly bowed. She was very much the disciplinarian, requiring everyone to "sit up straight" in their chairs. If you disobeyed, she would hit you on the palm of your hand with a ruler. Mrs. Tierny was my second-grade teacher. She seemed to be around Mrs. Child's age, but she was softer in her approach. She inspired us to be creative. She was open to our ideas and questions. She celebrated everyone's birthday with a cake. Miss Zolner was my third-grade teacher. She was strict. We were in her class to learn, and it was her job to make sure we did. I later discovered that she really cared about everyone doing really well. She wore her hair short and had round, rimless glasses. She was not married and lived with an older brother. She drove an old army green Studebaker.

LEFT TO RIGHT: Mrs. Shallenberger, Mrs. Hogan, Mrs. Hawes, Mrs. Carhart, Mr. Belotin, Mrs. Happy, Miss Avery, Miss Smith, Mr. McGrattan. SEATED: Miss Swart.

Grades, K-6

LEFT TO RIGHT: Mrs. Hunter, Mrs. Roberts, Mrs. Connolly, Miss Stackpole, Miss Zolner, Mrs. McNeil, Mrs. Connell, Mrs. Childs, Mrs. Kniffin, Mrs. Haskins, Miss Curran. SEATED: Miss Reynolds.

19

The school provided hot lunch for twenty-five cents and milk for three cents. However, most of the children brought their lunch and only occasionally purchased hot lunch. No one in my family could afford hot lunch except on the rare occasion when we saved money from beer bottles given to us by Mr. Brummy in exchange for going to Adamo's bar to pick up a bottle of beer for him. The children who brought their lunches usually brought baloney or peanut butter and jelly sandwiches on white bread. They also purchased milk. My lunch more often than not consisted of a homemade biscuit with homemade jam or margarine. Occasionally, we might have peanut butter and jelly on white bread. Our family would melt the peanut butter so it would spread thinner on the bread. That way, the jar would last longer. Sometimes if I had a biscuit for lunch, I would either eat by myself or throw my lunch away. I did not go to the lunchroom. I sometimes waited in the bathroom until others finished lunch and then went outside to play with them.

Mrs. Carhart was my fourth-grade teacher. She was a tall, sophisticated-looking woman around the age of Mrs. Childs. She always spoke in a tender but firm voice. I remember one incident in her class that had nothing to do with her as a teacher, but it brought me back to the reality of my environment. One day I was playing during recess with some of the other kids in class. A girl named Susan ran over to me, and I turned away from her, slightly brushing into her. She looked at me somewhat astonished. I said I was sorry and continued to play. The next day her older sister came to my class and told me that if I ever touch Susan again, she was going to beat me up. I was astonished! I didn't know what she was talking about, and she was getting angry because I didn't seem to know. I turned and walked away, wondering why she was talking to me in such harsh terms for accidentally touching someone. It was quite a while after the incident before it dawned on me why there was such a commotion.

The Coeymans School was overcrowded, and the school district decided to convert Beck's roller skating rink into classrooms for the fifth and sixth grades. Since there was a large space in the middle of the building, most of our recess took place indoors. If the weather was bad outside, we would sometimes have a dance after lunch. This presented problems because while the girls would dance with the other girls, only a few of the boys wanted to dance with the girls. Moreover, because my brother Eugene and I were the only two Negro boys, we took turns dancing with Betty Comithier, the only Negro girl. We did not want to get in trouble by trying to dance with a white girl.

Mrs. Nuite was my fifth-grade teacher. She turned out to be the strictest of all my teachers. It was traditional for the fifth- and sixth-grade classes to go on field trips. Mrs. Nuite would hear none of it. She refused to take us on any trips. Other classes in the building went on several trips. She constantly gave us tests based on her homework assignments. Yet she was a kind person who seemed to want the best for her students. We started out disliking her as a teacher and ended up admiring her for her desire to see all us become good students. Our lack of field trips became a badge of honor!

Mr. Prendergast was my sixth-grade and first male teacher. He had a reputation for being a tough disciplinarian. The alternative to him was Mrs. Beggs, who had a reputation for punching her students in the sides as part of her discipline. I found Mr. Prendergast to be an excellent teacher. However, I do recall the time he kicked me out of his class. One of the classmates was throwing paper. Mr. Prendergast caught him throwing the paper and decided that the whole class needed to be punished. We had to forgo recess and sit still at our desks the entire recess period. As we sat there, some kids began to look at one another, expressing body language that clearly implied that we found the whole thing quite amusing. I guess I had such a look. Mr. Prendergast looked at me, and after a couple of minutes, he told me to leave the room. I left the room and sat in the principal's office. Fortunately for me, the principal did not come out while I was there. Despite this strange incident, at the end of the year, I was quite surprised to see that I had gotten straight As in all subjects for the first time.

Although our school was over a mile away, we walked to school every day while other children rode the bus. Our school friends waived to us each morning as they road by us on the highway. During the winter we would get so cold that our hands hurt when we got next to the radiators at school. I got frostbite on my hands and feet, and I continue to live with those consequences today. I lose circulation in my hands and feet when they are exposed to cold. One day Mickey Gladney (the one who took my bike) got so cold while walking to school that she curled up on the side of the road. Fortunately, the music teacher, Mr. Duncan, was driving to school and picked her up. Shortly after the incident, we were permitted to ride the bus to school.

With eleven children in the family, we did not have much in the way of clothing. Much of what we had came from local white people who would give their old clothing to us. My sisters would get clothing from the various people for whom they worked. Some were generous and gave the clothing freely while others wanted my sisters to work in exchange for the clothing. My sister Sally worked for Rose Frangella, who had a son named Jimmy who was my age. She would give some of Jimmy's clothing to Sally. I would wear the clothes to school and sit next to Jimmy. Jimmy never said a word about the clothes.

Miss Zolner, my third-grade teacher, gave me a note to take home. The other kids saw her give me the note and convinced me that I was in trouble. I tore the note up and did not give it to my mother. After a few weeks, she asked me if my mother had said anything about the note. I said no. She gave me another note and told me to make sure I gave it to my mother. I think she suspected that I never gave my mother the other note. This time I gave the note to my mother and waited anxiously for my punishment, which I knew was sure to come. To my surprise, the note was simply an inquiry as to whether my mother would mind if Miss Zolner gave me some clothes to bring home. My mother said she would welcome the clothes, and Miss Zolner brought in several boxes over time.

Fishing in Coeymans Creek

In addition to farming, many of the people liked to fish in general, particularly in Coeymans Creek. The creek ran past the Frangella mushroom plant, through the Bottom, and down a series of falls and eventually flowed into the Hudson River. We used to dig worms and sell them in small cans in the community. We loved it when it rained because the big worms (night crawlers) would come to the surface. The red worms seem to hide under rotten wood and were much smaller. A can of worms could fetch at least twenty-five cents.

The people fished at all points along the creek. During heavy rains in the spring, the creek would overflow its banks and cause a lot of flooding in the Bottom. The creek also took a few lives over the course of time. Many of the children did not know how to swim and were told not to go near the creek. Unfortunately, some the adults died in the creek whether or not they knew how to swim.

One Saturday in April 1958, Jimmy Hunt was at our house. Mr. Ray came home from Adamo's and walked over to where Jimmy, my brother Eugene, and I were sitting. "Y'all want to go fishing?" he said. We did not really want to go since it was late afternoon and we would be eating soon, but we knew that Mr. Ray loved fishing and was a good fisherman.

Besides, the creek was just down the hill in back of the house. We walked with Mr. Ray back to his house and waited while he got his fishing tackle and pole. For some reason, he also put on a big overcoat. We didn't have fishing poles. We intended to skip rocks instead. We soon reached the creek bank, and Mr. Ray walked on ahead of us where he could fish without our rock skipping disturbing the fish he wanted to catch. A short time later, we heard a splash and wondered what had happened. Then we heard someone coughing and the noise of someone swimming. We ran up toward where Mr. Ray was standing and saw him in the creek, but he was struggling to swim with the coat on. Jimmy lunged forward, but we held him back from jumping in the water. "Let me go. Let me go," Jimmy screamed.

"You aren't big enough to help him," Gene and I said almost in unison.

"Let's get some help. Run up the hill now," we said and took off toward the house.

"Mama, Mr. Ray's in the creek. Somebody gotta help him!" I exclaimed.

She said, "Go get Tommy (Wilson). He can swim." Tommy lived next door, and we took off over to his house, yelling, "Help. Help. Mr. Ray fell in the creek!" Tommy was dressing to go out for the evening. When he heard us yelling, he took off running in his dress clothes for the creek and dove in immediately at the spot we last saw Mr. Ray. Meanwhile, someone at Tommy's house called the fire department.

It was now dusk and getting difficult to see. Tommy could not locate Mr. Ray and got out of the water once the fire department arrived. We began to shiver as the night air seemed to grow cold, but it was also because we became afraid. We did not understand what had just taken place or what was sure to follow. We had witnessed someone die. The fire department searched well into the night. Ms. Sylvester came home from church, and Jimmy went over to her house. Gene and I went to bed. Sometime in the middle of the night, I felt someone was shaking me, and I soon realize it was Jimmy. He was crying. I asked, "Did they find him?"

"Yes," he answered. "My grandpa drowned." We just looked at each other without knowing what more to say.

Charlie Logan used to fish in the creek in the Bottom in back of his house. He lived with his mother, Rosa Logan, and often kept company with Miss Nellie Mae after her husband, Garland Turner, died. Miss Nellie Mae was also quite good at fishing. She would sit on the creek bank for hours on end, reeling in perches and suckers. A couple of houses over from Miss Nellie lived Mr. Ben and Miss Bee. Both of them often fished in the creek among other places. Miss Bee rivaled Miss Nellie for her fishing prowess.

Across the creek from the Bottom was the housing for the men who worked at the Frangella mushroom plant. Some of them would also fish in the creek from the other side. One evening while fishing in the creek, Herman Gladney fell into the creek and drowned. He didn't know how to swim. Herman was a younger brother of Lightning (James Gladney) and Thunder (Edward "Willie" Gladney). He had come to Coeymans from Virginia. It seemed that tragedy followed the family. Thunder had been severely injured in a car accident while speeding on Route 9J. Confined to a wheelchair, he was returned home to Virginia. Garland Turner (Miss Nellie Mae's husband) and one other person were killed in the accident.

My father fished in the part of the creek near the rocks known as the Sucker Hole, where one could catch suckers (a fish that looks somewhat like a trout). John Henry and German would go with my father to fish.

Sometimes Cliff went along as well. Gene and I didn't usually go, and if we did, we didn't have a pole to put in the water. John, German, and Cliff became avid fishermen.

My father carried a five-gallon pail with him to put the fish in. It seems that everyone participated in cleaning the fish when he brought them home. The bullhead fish found in the Hudson River were particularly difficult to clean. The fish does not have scales, and it has to be skinned by using pliers to clip the skin and then pull it off while holding the fish by the head. The fish has very sharp tentacles around the head that invariable pierced your hands when you held the fish by the head.

Wintertime in Coeymans

In our house there were lots of chores for everyone. Key to our winter survival was an adequate supply of wood in the woodshed and on the back porch. Every year my father would literally chop down small forests with an ax. He later purchased a chain saw. The wood was hauled by truck to our yard, where my uncle Green would help us saw it up. My uncle had an old 1936 Plymouth that had been modified into a jeep with no rear end. The jeep was used solely in the fall months as a power source to turn a leather belt on a circle saw. My uncle would go down in the Bottom as well as around the Hill to set up the saw to cut up wood for the families. He would charge a modest fee for his services. My uncle had a rack on which the logs were laid and then fed to the saw. The logs were cut in short lengths to fit in the woodstoves. When he cut our wood, we would help load the wood onto the saw rack. Some of the logs were quite large. We would later use an iron wedge and a sledgehammer to split the sawed logs. The wood was then stacked in the woodshed and on the back porch. The remainder of the year the jeep would sit in our backyard, rusting away. We would climb upon the jeep and pretend to drive it. We knew that without the battery, it was not going anywhere.

The jeep also sat in the middle of our basketball court. A ball that bounced off the jeep was called out of bounds.

In addition to the logs for the woodstoves, we had to cut up dry wood or kindling that would be used to start the fires in the stoves. This wood would also be stored in the woodshed for use in the winter. Sometimes my father would also order a ton of coal to burn in the potbelly stove.

The water was a special problem in the winter. A fifty-gallon barrel cut open at both ends was usually placed around the hydrant and filled with straw to provide insulation. This kept the hydrant from freezing up except when the temperature dropped below zero. If the hydrant froze, we had to build a fire around it to thaw it out. Sometimes this took quite a while to accomplish. We often got cold while trying to thaw out the hydrant. We could not go to school unless the hydrant was working. We needed the water for the day.

Coeymans always seemed quite cold in the winter. The temperatures were nearly always below zero, and the snow often drifted to the bottom of our windows, averaging one to six feet at times. The wood stacked on the porch or stored in the woodshed was worth its weight in gold! We just needed to shovel out paths to the woodshed to get the wood and the coal. We also shoveled paths to the meat house, the water hydrant, and the outhouse. My uncle had a car. He would wait for the town snowplow truck to come down the highway and ask him to run through the yard so he could get out to Route 144.

The windows on the house did not have weather stripping to seal them. Instead we cut up pieces of plastic and nailed them around the windows on the front of the house. We had wood doors on the windows in the back of the house. In snow storms and on very cold days, we would shut the doors on the windows to keep in the heat. My father would put coal in the stove at night to keep a fire going all night. Sometimes the stove would get red all over from the extreme heat generated by the coal. Eventually, it would burn down, and the stove would cool down as the night wore on. It was not uncommon for one of the children to get burned for getting too close to the stove. I got burned on my stomach and forearm when I got pushed into the stove while playing hide-and-seek.

We would close off the dining room and kitchen at night in order to keep the heat in the bedrooms. As a result, the water in the pails on the shelf in the kitchen would be frozen solid in the morning. We would start a fire in the kitchen stove and sit the water pails on the stove to thaw out.

The winter was not all hard times. We had lots of fun building snowmen and igloos. The snow was so high that we could build igloos that lasted a couple of weeks. We also loved to go sleigh riding. We would ride from the top of the Hill down into the Bottom. All the kids who lived on the Hill and in the Bottom would participate. When the snow was deep, we usually had the day off from school. On those days we would ride sleighs all day long. Those of us who did not have sleighs would use cardboard boxes. When we got home, we would get snow off the roof of the woodshed so Mama could make some snow cream with Pet canned milk, sugar, and vanilla extract flavoring. You had to eat it fast because the snow would melt quickly.

THE WAY WE WERE
1957–62

Softball Fields

Everyone seemed to play softball—girls and boys. We would play in the space between the fourth and the third house on the Hill. The field was essentially dirt and gravel. We would set up base lines and bags that fit the yard even though they weren't up to any regulation. The people who lived on the Hill would play every day. Sometimes children would come up from the Bottom to play. Every now and then, someone would hit a ball so hard that it would break a window in the Wilson's house, which happened to be right center field. Route 144 was left field.

When we played in the Bottom, we used the open field across the road from Aunt Mary's house. It was much bigger than the spot used on the Hill. The softball teams were ad hoc. Whenever we could get enough players together, we'd chose teams and play. We usually played after supper around six o'clock or so. Earl Brewer and Leonard Comithier Jr. were probably the oldest in the group. However, sometimes McKinley Jones Jr., William Lipscomb (we called him Pan), Bobby Hughes, and Lawrence Brewer would also play. From the Comithier family, we also had Mickey (Eugene), Perry, and Avery. Sometimes Betty and Arlene would play. Tony Kittle and Billy Stevens were among the youngest players. Clifford, Eugene, and I also played.

As we got older, we tended to play most of our games at the church. The field at the church was sort of narrow. A left-handed person would regularly hit the ball into the roadway and toward Coeymans Creek, and a right-handed person would hit the ball into the woods on the hillside. In addition to the usual players, the boys in the Wyche family, who lived in New Baltimore, sometimes came up to play. From the Wyche family, we had Ray, Jay, Guy, and Larry. Sometimes Billy Stevens's cousins Harry and Tiny (Edward Jr.) would come up from Coxsackie and play. When the Boldens lived in Coeymans, Richard, James, and Larry would also play.

The summers in Coeymans were often very hot. Negro children did not go to summer camp. Fortunately, the church had some summer activities. We would do arts and crafts during the heat of the day. Boys and girls would make such items as potholders and ceramics with Bible verses. There was a grove of trees at the end of the softball field where everyone gathered at tables and benches. We often made up songs to sing while working or just sitting around. The girls would skip rope and alternately press their hands together in cadence with the songs.

As we got older, many of the boys also played Little League, Babe Ruth, and American Legion baseball. Nonetheless, we would get together and play softball when we could. Sometimes we would go down to New Baltimore to visit the Wyche's. They preferred to play baseball. We would play on the local Little League field. More often than not, we did not have enough people to field two full teams. As a result, we would play with a shared catcher and call our own balls and strikes. My brother Cliff, who was known to be an excellent Little League baseball player, often batted left-handed (as opposed to his normal right-handed stance) in his teenage years as a way of evening out the strength of the teams.

I was always in between the older and younger group of players. Tony, Perry, and Billy saw me as the older of their peer group, and Leonard, Cliff, Mickey, and the Wyches saw me as the younger of their peer group. One day in a baseball game, the way I was regarded came through in a dramatic way. I was on a team that was losing the ball game because we had the weaker team. We were playing in New Baltimore on a Little League field that had a fence. The older boys kept knocking the ball over the fence. We had already lost two baseballs, and we were down to our last ball. I came up to bat with two people on base. I could feel the anxiety of Tony and Perry on my team. They wanted Jay Wyche or Cliff to be at the plate. A two-base hit would tie the game. If I made an out, the game would be over. I don't recall the count when I swung at a fastball. All I know was that I could see it very well and swung from my heels. The ball not only went over the fence but kept going high into the air and into the forest that was quite a distance beyond the fence. Everyone was stunned! Tony jumped up and down and met me at home plate with several slaps on the back. He could not stop talking. Mickey, who was on the other team, turned away from the fence and walked off the field. Everyone slowly followed in disbelief. No one went to retrieve the ball. I am sure it is still in the woods all these many years later.

Working for a Living

I began working outside the house when I was nine years old. All my older brothers and sisters worked outside the house. Sally and John quit school and went to work. German, Mary Lee, Pearl, Cliff, and Gene all had jobs working for the Frangellas, the Mayones, or just odd jobs around town. Gene had an enterprising newspaper route, which included carrying *numbers* for some people. My father did not make a lot of money, and we needed to work to buy school supplies and clothes and also to have a little spending money. We also put food on the family table, especially in the winter months when the brickyard closed down and my father was on unemployment.

The Motens

I worked for John and Susie Moten, the oldest Negro people in Coeymans. Mrs. Moten, a small built and quiet woman, was the *mother* of Riverview Missionary Baptist Church. John Moten was a short, rotund man who wore a "cough drop" hat and sometimes smoked a pipe or a cigar. He suffered from a number of ailments and always seemed to have trouble breathing. He used to work for the railroad, but I didn't know him until he was retired. Mrs. Moten was older, but she continued to do housework for the Suderlys.

Mrs. Moten was the kindest person one could ever meet. She always seemed at peace and never seemed to get upset except on occasion with Mr. Moten. Mr. Moten, on the other hand, always seemed angry about one thing or the other. I met him when I was nine years old when he asked me to carry firewood into the house for him. The Motens cooked and heated their home by woodstoves. Mr. Moten would chop wood during the day, and after school I would stack the wood upon the porch for them so that it was easy to retrieve.

At first, Mr. Moten would give me a quarter to bring in the wood for him. After a while, I became a regular and Mrs. Moten would give me a dollar at the end of each week. She would also give me a bag of candy on Saturday. Sometimes when I finished the wood, they would ask me to sit for a spell, and I would watch television with them. We didn't have one at home at the time. Once I was so nervous sitting with them that I started talking and couldn't stop (or so it seemed). Finally, Mrs. Moten said to me in her usual quite way, "Son, did anyone ever tell you that a still tongue will make a wise head?" I was totally embarrassed and looked for a way to leave quietly.

I didn't like Mr. Moten, but I wanted the money and the candy. At the time, it was the only work I could get. He always seemed to be trying to get more work out of me than he was willing to pay for. Fortunately, Mrs. Moten would see this sometimes and would give me a little extra. I recall quite vividly my experience with Mr. Moten's garden.

In the past, Mr. Moten would have the garden dug up by Mitch Stevens, who would do it with his tractor and charge for it. Mr. Moten got the idea that he would have me dig it up by hand for less. He told me that digging up the garden would be extra work and that he would pay me out of his pension check when it came. Every day after school, I would work on the garden by hand until after about a week or so I got it dug up and ready for planting. The garden was big, and I had done all I could do to finish it. I knew for sure I was going to get at least five dollars and maybe a little extra for my work. Mr. Moten as much as said so with his constant promise of "big money."

When Mr. Moten got his pension check, he gave me a dollar! I was so disappointed that I froze. I didn't know what to do. I never thought he would do that to me. I knew that I could not argue with him because my mother would probably whip me for sassing back a grown person. I wanted to cry but managed to force myself to extend my hand toward him to return the dollar. I believe I managed to say through the tears, "If this is all you think the job was worth, then you can have it back!" He was irate and started to raise his voice. "You ain't no man. You can't get paid like a man!" With tears now running down my face, I said that I had worked hard to dig up the garden and should be paid more for my work. At that point, Mrs. Moten came out on the porch where this conversation was taking place and gave me another dollar and said that I should go home. I never knew whether she was upset at me. I felt bad because I respected her and didn't want her to think ill of me. I did continue to bring in the wood, but it was not the same. Eventually, I stopped. I never told my mother why I stopped.

The Little Painter

The Suttons

Mrs. Sutton, the wife of Rev. Samuel Sutton, the pastor at Riverview Missionary Baptist Church, was visiting our house when she saw me painting our living room. She remarked that she had some painting to do at the parsonage. Subsequently, she asked me whether I'd do some painting for her at the parsonage. I had no prior training, but I was always very neat and liked to get things done right. I observed Albert Nino, the old Italian man who lived near the church and worked as a professional housepainter.

I was asked to paint a bathroom in the parsonage. I showed up for work and had only shortly begun when I heard Mrs. Sutton having an argument with Helena, her stepdaughter. It got pretty rough for a child of my age. I didn't know that kind of conversation took place in a pastor's house. After the argument, which went on for quite a while, Helena came into the bathroom and told me not to say anything about the argument. I didn't know what to say. I was afraid to say anything. I looked at her, said nothing, lowered my head as if in acquiescence, and returned to my painting.

Nana Coles

Mrs. Sutton told Mrs. Nana Coles, a houseguest, about my painting. Mrs. Coles was a retired lawyer who lived with the Suttons, although she had a house in Catskill on the Hudson River. There was a church picnic coming up in July, and there was a charge for riding the church bus if you were not a member of the church. I was not a member. We didn't have a car in our family. Nor was there any money to send me on the picnic. Mrs. Coles said she liked my painting at the Sutton's house and asked me if I wanted to paint at her house to make some money to go on the picnic. Mrs. Sutton said she would take me down to Mrs. Coles's house.

The church had sponsored retreats to Mrs. Coles's house. Rumor had it that Mrs. Coles was terminally ill and was expected to leave her house to the church or to the Suttons. As it turned out, neither event happened reportedly because Mrs. Coles and the Suttons subsequently had a falling out.

Mrs. Sutton took me down to Mrs. Coles's house in Catskill. It was a stately old white house, which stood on the opposite side of the road from the Hudson River with a little cabana across the road on the riverbank. It was a place with a cool breeze. Unfortunately, I was the only person there besides Mrs. Coles.

Mrs. Coles was very particular about painting. I believe she was a little skeptical about my ability given that I was about eleven years old at the time. She wanted me to paint all the trim in the house with enamel paint. I hated enamel paint! It was oily and streaky. The brush would always lose hairs and you have to remove the hairs from the surface with your hands. I was determined to get it right. So I set about setting up the job. I taped everything with masking tape to avoid getting paint on the areas that were not to be painted. I selected the smaller brush because I was able to better control it.

Trimming always took a long time. I started about nine thirty in the morning. I stopped at one o'clock for a half-hour lunch break. I ate my sandwich in the cabana across the street. I resumed painting and continued until about six o'clock, when she gave me supper. I thought I was finished for the day. However, since there was no one else there to talk to or play with, I went back to work until it was dark. She didn't want me to paint in the dark, because she thought I might skip some spots. When I stopped for the evening, I could barely move. I wanted desperately to go home. Until that day, I do not think I ever stayed overnight at anyone's house.

The next morning I got up early. I did not have a toothbrush or change of clothes. I washed my face and combed my hair with a comb in the bathroom. Since Ms. Coles was not yet awake, I sat in the cabana on the riverbank for a while. I started to paint again about eight o'clock. Mrs. Coles got up a little later and asked if I wanted breakfast. I am sure I had breakfast. I can't recall what it was. At that point, I wanted to be sure to finish so Mrs. Sutton could come and pick me up to go home. I painted all day and soon realized that I would not finish until early evening. I thought that perhaps Mrs. Sutton could pick me up by suppertime. As it turned out, I finished by suppertime, but Mrs. Sutton didn't come down. I finished cleaning up the brushes and put things away. That evening I sat in the cabana. I was so lonely and angry. I wanted to go home! I am sure Mrs. Coles could tell by my demeanor that I was upset. There was little or no conversation at the dinner table. Mrs. Sutton came the next morning and eventually took me home. Mrs. Sutton (rather than Mrs. Coles) paid me twelve dollars. I gave her some of it back to pay for my seat on the picnic bus.

Pauline Sutton

Mrs. Sutton told her daughter Pauline about my painting. Pauline, a schoolteacher, lived on Hall Place in Albany. At the time, it was a rather exclusive address for Negro people in Albany. Pauline asked me to come up to Albany and paint her living room. This was great! I'd make a lot of money—whatever a lot meant at the time.

I had to go to Albany by myself on a bus and then walk to Pauline's house. I had been to Albany before to get my haircut, but that was downtown on Green Street, not across State Street and into the Arbor Hill area. I didn't have any paint clothes or painting tools for that matter. I just got on the Mountain View bus and took it to State and North Pearl Streets in Albany. I walked north on North Pearl Street to Clinton Avenue and went up Clinton Avenue to Ten Broeck Street, turned right, walked to Second Street, turned left, and then walked to Hall Place. Hall Place was behind St. Joseph's Church between Second Street and Ten Broeck Place. As I walked to Pauline's house, I was so scared that I thought everyone was staring at me. I just kept my head down and kept walking rather fast.

When I arrived at Pauline's house, she told me she wanted her living room painted. She gave me the paint, the roller, the brushes, and the drop cloths. Then she left. I had no idea when she would be returning or what she expected to see when she got back. I turned the radio on and opened the windows. It never occurred to me to check out the apartment while I was there. I guess my upbringing was such that nothing in my character would lead me to rummage through someone's house. Instead I set about painting.

It was on this job that I started to develop painting techniques. I covered the roller pan with the plastic from dry cleaning so that I didn't get the roller pan dirty. For the edging of the ceiling and high areas, I tied my brush to a broom handle so I could manage from the floor without a ladder. I also tied the roller to the broom handle to be able to roll from a standing position on the floor. I moved all the furniture to the center of the room and covered it up. This left me free to work around the room without the impediment of furniture. Although she didn't ask me, I actually painted the room twice because the first coat didn't cover very well.

When she returned that early evening, I was all done with everything all cleaned up. She paid me, and I headed for the bus stop. I forget the amount I got paid, but I remember I felt really rich. I had an extra bounce in my step. I knew I could get both soda and candy and have some money left over. As I walked to the bus stop, I became anxious because I didn't want to get robbed. After all, I just got paid. I didn't know what to do. I walked faster. I also thought everyone was staring at me again. As I boarded the bus at the bus terminal at Broadway and State Street, I was glad once again to be headed home to Coeymans.

Mattie Hill

Pauline's hairdresser lived around the corner on Ten Broeck Place. She told the owner, Mattie Hill, about my paint job. Mattie asked Pauline to have me come to see her. Once again, I found myself aboard a Mountain View bus headed to Albany to do some painting. This time things were a little different. By then I knew I was a pretty good painter and wanted to get paid a little more. Mattie wanted me to paint two full rooms and a hallway. This was going to take several days because of the extensive trim work. I told Mattie that I would charge one dollar an hour. This would be premium rate by comparison to the seventy-five cents an hour my brothers and sisters were getting for doing housework on Frangella Avenue in Coeymans. Mattie agreed, and I began the job. The job proved to be bigger than I thought. I had trouble with the ceilings, the stairway, and the trim. After two days work (about sixteen dollars), she asked me to reduce my rate. I was shocked! I thought she would increase my pay, not ask me to take a pay cut. I agreed to finish the job at seventy-five cents an hour. I could have slowed down and gotten the same pay, but I decided it was best just to finish and get out as soon as possible. I knew I was being taken advantage of, but I didn't know what to do about it. Mattie told Pauline she thought I was a "wonderful little painter."

Geneva Kittle

As it happened, Geneva Kittle also went to Mattie's for her hair treatments. Geneva was the mother of one of my best friends, Tony. Tony's parents were divorced. His father, George, was the son of the man who owned Kittles Bar and Grill on North Swan Street. It was one of the places for Negro people to go for some nightlife. It featured live entertainment. Although Tony lived in Coeymans with his grandmother, Eva Leigh, he sometimes came to Albany on weekends to stay with his mother. Mattie told Tony's mother about my painting, and when I was at her mother's house playing monopoly with Tony, she asked me if I would do some painting for her. I said yes.

Tony was in Albany the weekend that I was supposed to paint. I came up by bus and walked to 82 Hamilton Street. Mrs. Kittle was not at home, but she had left the paint materials that I needed. When I rang the doorbell, I awakened Tony. It was strange because I had never been to his house in Albany. We always played monopoly at his grandmother's house. Also, Tony had never seen me paint or anything that I had painted. I believe he was a bit skeptical as well. After all, I was only two years older than Tony and had been painting for at least two years now. He did not know how to paint.

His mother wanted the living room painted one color—beige. This room only had natural light from the street side of the apartment. It was dim without the lights on. I began painting, and Tony began watching. The wet paint made the room appear even darker. We talked a lot about everything, but I noticed Tony was a bit anxious. About halfway around the room, the paint started to dry in some places but was not completely dry. This made the room look like it had blotches. By this time, I knew Tony was getting concerned. I told him not worry.

Around noon Mrs. Kittle called Tony and asked him how it was going. He said it was going all right except that the paint looks really dark. She asked him to put me on the telephone. I explained to her that the paint was not dry and that it would lighten up as it dried. She seemed worried, but she said okay.

I continued to paint and finished about four thirty in the afternoon. Half the room was dry, the other half wet. I cleaned up the room and put the furniture back as the paint continued to dry. At around six in the evening, the paint was substantially dry, and the room really looked great. Mrs. Kittle came home shortly thereafter and was pleasantly surprised. Tony said he didn't know what happened, but the room changed after the paint dried. That evening Tony's uncle Arthur and his wife (Mildred, I believe) came by and took us all out to dinner. After that, I took the 9:50 p.m. Mountain View bus (also known and incorrectly referred to as the Ten-ten) back to Coeymans.

The Adamos

I also worked for Marie Adamo, Joe's wife, on Saturdays. She wanted me to wash windows and floors. I will always remember the "famous fifty" windows she had in her parlor. I would wash them inside and out (weather permitting) almost every week. She would stand on an angle to be sure there were no streaks. I also had to wash her floors with two pails of water, one with a light soap and the other to rinse. I did this routine also almost every week, for about two years, from eight thirty to noon, followed sometimes by lunch. She was a very nice woman who treated me very well. One time her best of intentions came off as naively offensive. She said to me in a very thoughtful voice, "Jimmy, we had a wonderful ham last night for dinner. We had some leftovers for the dog, but I knew you were coming, so I saved them for you." Somewhat taken aback at that moment, I could only offer a polite thank-you.

Jack of All Trades

As far as I can remember, I've always been inquisitive about how things worked or are created. I often observed my uncle Green working around the house, Mr. Nino painting, or Tommy Wilson working in his TV repair shop in the back of his house. It did not take me long to figure out what they were doing and also to think of ways to improve the process. I seemed to see things beyond what was apparent and realize what was possible. In this regard, I had a number of projects of my own.

I would watch my mother wallpaper, paint, and lay linoleum. I soon realized that I could do the same thing. I was a stickler for *getting it right*. I was soon able to handle these chores and looked forward to them. It seemed that because the linoleum was inferior and being placed on well-worn wooden floors, we were replacing the linoleum every six months or so. I liked the idea of custom cutting the linoleum. I also like custom fitting the wallpaper, matching every piece to the other. For me, there was a sense of accomplishment if I could make it come out right.

The front porch on our house had rotted away. My mother replaced it with the back of an upright piano that we had in the house. We had decided to dispose of the piano once we heard it playing at night with no one playing it. Our neighbors had big fully screened porches on which to sit. I was determined to build us a porch like theirs. We had some wood that had been dropped off at our house as kindling that looked pretty good for building. I had no idea how much wood I would need to build the porch. Nonetheless, I started the project. I worked one whole day and couldn't seem to make much progress. My neighbor stopped by to ask what I was doing. It was not a serious question, just a taunt by a supposed adult. I took off the next several days from school and was able to get two upright posts in place and to double the size of the platform for the porch. That was as far as I got with the project. I didn't have any more wood. Shortly thereafter, there came the news that the new owners of the company houses were going to tear down all the houses and build new ones. Eventually, they did the former but not the latter.

Church Picnics

Each year the church would sponsor a picnic for members and nonmembers. The picnics were usually held at Caroga Lake, New York, or at Central Park in Schenectady, New York. The picnic was one of *the* events of the year. The old and young alike looked forward to the picnic. The church would charter buses to take church members to the picnic site. As a nonmember, I had to pay a fee and did not get to go often. While Mary Lee, Pearl, and Cliff had joined the church and usually went on the picnic, Eugene and I had not joined, and we often didn't have the money to pay for the bus. Nor was their enough food for a picnic basket for all of us. We would stay home with Mama and our younger sisters. It seemed as if the whole town was abandoned. Hardly anybody was left in town, and it was traumatic to see the buses go by without us with our friends waving to us out the window. Our dream was to get a job so we would have the money to get on the bus for the picnic.

As we got older, Eugene joined the church. He also had a paper route along with other odd jobs that brought him enough money so that he could go on the picnic among other things. The only work I could get were my painting jobs. Later I started to work for Marie Adamo and John Moten. I could now go on the picnic. I never did join that church. My mother and father never went on the picnic. They would stay home with my younger sisters.

The picnic was a *happening* for everyone. The women would prepare their best meals, including barbecue ribs and chicken, potato and macaroni salads, deviled eggs, corn on the cob, mustard greens, and baked beans. The desserts included berry, sweet potato and rhubarb pies, cakes, and melons. Each family would prepare baskets. At the picnic site, everyone would sit in the same area and spread out their baskets. Billy Steven's aunt Catherine was an incredible cook. She would always come prepared to feed the neighborhood, and the neighborhood always wanted to taste what she had prepared. For the most part, everyone would share the meal. There were some who seemed to think sharing was not a good idea and limited their sharing to members of their extended families. Nonetheless, this was generally a time of good feelings among all.

Caroga Lake seemed to have many activities for children and adults. We particularly liked the bumper cars. There was a chance to swim, but most of us did not know how to swim. There were rides and playgrounds. The big event was softball. The young men would always play a game in the midafternoon, and everyone seemed to gather around to watch. After the game it was time for the desserts! Watermelons were everywhere.

Hog-Killin' Time

From May through November, Negroes on the Hill and in the Bottom raised pigs. We often fed our pigs leftover bread my father retrieved from the town dump mixed with pig feed. It was interesting to see them grow from a bit larger than piglets to full-grown pigs by November. November was the month when everyone slaughtered pigs just ahead of the onset of winter so that the meat could be stored in the meat house outside. It seemed that every Saturday somebody was slaughtering pigs. We would slaughter our pigs on the Saturday after Thanksgiving.

My father had a stroke in 1959, and we were in a quandary as to what to do about the pigs. Several of his friends said they would come by and help with the slaughtering. Kelly Banks, who lived in the Bottom, came by and offered to help. As usual, we set the Saturday after Thanksgiving as the date for killing the pigs. About a week before the scheduled date, Kelly Banks set up a scalding box near his house even though he did not have any pigs. We thought he might be buying some pigs to slaughter. One evening we heard our pigs squealing in the pigpen and ran to the door to see what was wrong. The light from the door disclosed two men in the pigpen trying to wrestle the pigs to the ground. My father said, "Bring me my gun. I am gonna shoot whoever is out there." As Cliff went to get the 12-gauge shotgun, the men jumped over the back fence of the pigpen and ran down toward the Bottom. When my father got the gun, he fired a couple of rounds into the air to make sure the men knew he intended to shoot them. The next day, the scalding tub that was in Kelly Banks's yard was gone, and Kelly, according to Blanche, his wife, was out of town.

Slaughtering pigs required many things. First, you needed a scalding box in which to heat the water. My uncle Green had one of these. We would dig a trench about two feet deep and fill it with hardwood and kindling for the fire needed to heat the water. On the day of the slaughter, the scalding box would be set on the trench and filled with water, and someone would light the fire. My father would add some lye to the water to help loosen the hair on the pigs.

Second, you needed a strong crew that could wrestle the hogs down and hold them in place while the slaughter took place. A person needed to reach under the body of the pig and pull the hind leg from the opposite side. This would turn the pig over on its back. The legs of the pig would then have to be quickly restrained by men holding them in place. The actual slaughter was a specialty. It was important that the pig bled externally and not internally. Knives were specially sharpened to easily cut the throat of the pig and quickly sever the aorta. My father was pretty good at sticking the pigs, but Mr. Paul and my uncle Green were probably the best at it. Mr. Paul seemed to know exactly where to cut and how long an incision to make. He was a surgeon with the knife. The pig would usually bleed out in just a few minutes.

Next, the slaughtered pig was placed on ropes in the scalding water and rolled around for a few minutes. The men would then use their knives to scrape off the hair until the pig was pink. It was necessary to hang the pig upside down by its hind feet on a wooden rack. My father would construct the rack supported by two A-braced posts. A wooden pole would be placed between the hind legs of the pig, which were supported only by the tendons in the back of the legs. Once the pigs are hanged, Mr. Paul or my uncle Green would then begin the disembowelment process. This required a steady hand. They didn't want to cut the intestines. Then they could remove all the organs from the pig.

We used the entire pig. The liver, the brains, the lungs (pluck and plender), the kidneys, and the intestines (chitterlings or chitlins) were all edible. The chitlins were the biggest chore. One had to pour hot water through segments until they were clean. The fat was then removed from the chitlins. The chitlins were left to soak overnight and then cleaned again before they were either boiled or fried. The fat from the chitlins was boiled down to make lard. The residue was used to make cracklin' bread.

We did not have a freezer. All the meat had to be salted down for the winter. A day or two after the pigs were slaughtered, we'd bring them into the house and lay them out on newspaper on the floor. My mother and father would then cut up the pigs. There were the hams and the shoulders. The midsection was cut into chunks to be boiled down for lard. The section normally used in stores for bacon was cut up so that we could ground it up for sausage. The pig head and pig feet were separated. All of the meat was then salted and placed in a saltbox in the woodshed. The sausage was heavily seasoned and stuffed into muslin bags and hung in the woodshed. Sometimes but not often my father would burn some hickory wood in the woodshed and hang the hams and shoulders over the smoke for several days. The meat did not spoil because of the salt and the cold weather.

The pig meat would last through the winter. As the winter wore on, it was necessary to soak the meat to remove the salt before it was cooked. The hams were usually eaten at Christmas and New Year. The sausage didn't last very long. In fact, many of the men who helped with the slaughter usually looked forward to receiving a bag of sausage in addition to the potato wine they drank liberally during the slaughtering process.

The Clambake

Once a year in the summer, the Suderlys would sponsor a clambake for all the employees at the brickyard. There would be an ample supply of corn on the cob, clams, hamburgers, and hot dogs. All the men would come, and some would bring their male children. Women and female children were not allowed. The clambake would start about ten in the morning and last virtually all day. It was the one day that Joe Adamo didn't need to open his bar until after six in the evening.

We would show up at the clambake. No one seemed to notice us. We just ate everything in sight. The men were consuming beer and hard liquor. We had plenty of soft drinks. This was the one event where Negroes and whites came together for a social event. There was lots of laughing and joke telling. It was an all-around good time by all.

Monopoly

I don't recall how we started playing monopoly, but we became obsessed with the game one summer. Tony Kittle, Billy Stevens, Perry Comithier, Jimmy Gladney, my brother Eugene, and I were the main players. Tony had the game at his grandmother's house, where he stayed in Coeymans.

Every day in the summer, save Sunday, we would go down to Tony's house at about eight thirty in the morning to play. We would drift in one at a time over a period of about one hour until we'd all arrive. Tony was sometimes still in his pajamas. He would get dressed and eat breakfast while we were setting up the game.

We all knew the rules of the game. However, we would make up a few rules to make the game more interesting or to keep people in the game longer. For example, we decided to award the money collected for fines to whoever stopped on free parking. We would also make personal loans by collecting money owed on a delayed basis so that a player wouldn't have to mortgage property. Sometimes we created tensions by favoring one player over the over. These tensions never seemed to last long or prevent us from playing the next day.

Once school started, we could only play on Saturdays. Sundays were reserved for church. Everyone regularly went to Sunday school except me. Often while playing monopoly at Tony's house, his grandmother, a very religious woman known to thank God on a moment's notice for everything, would come home from work and ask, "Who goes to Sunday school?" Tony and Perry would start to laugh because they knew that I probably was the one person who had not gone to Sunday school. As we got older and started to work at odd jobs, the monopoly time waned and eventually stopped.

Berries and Greens

The summertime was always special in Coeymans. Most of the people we knew had gardens. The produce from the garden helped to supplement food on the table. Several people also canned their produce to provide for the winter. My father would dig up several plots of land owned by Sutton & Suderly by hand to plant corn, string beans, tomatoes, beets, carrots, cabbage, squash, turnips, and peppers. We had a garden near the house, one across the highway, and one down the hill near Coeymans Creek. He spent considerable time clearing the land, planting, and weeding. Some people in town had smaller showcase gardens. Mr. Paul always had a showcase. He had the best-looking tomatoes and strawberries. Others would use tractors to plow the land. Mr. Mitchell and his son Mick had several tractors that they used to plow their land and the land of others. In the latter years, when my father was no longer able to dig the gardens by hand, he would ask Mick to plow for us.

Strawberries, raspberries, and blackberries grew naturally around the area. We found *berry patches* on the hills above the brickyard and in the fields behind Wildy Pounds' house. Mustard greens and watercress (creasy) also grew naturally. We would pick the berries to make pies and jams. We sold some of the berries to others for twenty-five to thirty-five cents a pint. The mustard greens were in high demand. Many families would purchase bags of the greens from us. They used them at home, or more often than not, they used them to prepare dinners to be sold at Riverview Church or other churches in Albany. It was quite common for churches to raise funds by selling dinners. Some of the ladies in town would fix dinners on Friday for some of the brickyard men. They would eat the dinners at Adamo's after Joe cashed their paychecks.

The mustard greens seemed to grow everywhere, but seemed to do particularly well the closer they grew to the outhouses. We would pick the greens from the usual places but save the ones from near the outhouses to be on top of the bag. The bags would look particularly good with the big leafy greens on top. Miss Sylvester, our neighbor and grandmother to our friend Jimmy Hunt, would request a large order of greens every week. She belonged to Wilborn Temple First Church of God and Christ, a Pentecostal church in Albany. They prepared meals on Saturday to be sold on Sunday afternoon. She caught on to our scheme. She requested that we not include any greens that were picked near the outhouses. We agreed to her request, but we did not always honor it. We moved the leafy greens to the bottom of the bag for her.

Green and Frances Motley

Green and Frances Motley, my uncle and aunt, lived upstairs in the fourth house on the Hill. All their children were older than me. "Ung" Green, as we called him, was a fair-skinned man with a medium build who stood five feet ten inches tall. He wore glasses and always had a close haircut. He was my mother's oldest brother by their mother, Annie Lipford. He came to Coeymans in the 1920s where he met and married Frances Goods. He came to the ministry in response to a *call* by God he said he had received while tending to his garden. We would jokingly say he heard a crow screech, and it sounded like "Green go preach."

Ung Green was a quiet man who regularly carried his Bible. While he sometimes worked two jobs by day and by night, he also kept busy working around his house. Sunday, however, was a day for church and rest. A man of many skills, adept at masonry and carpentry, he installed electricity in his flat, sheet-rocked the walls, painted and wallpapered, and laid linoleum on the floors. He built his woodsheds, pigpen, chicken coup, garage, and outhouse—all of excellent quality. He also fixed his cars and repaired his gardening tools.

Since he did not go to work on the brickyard until seven in the morning, he would often come downstairs in the morning to talk with my mother. He never said much to us as children. From time to time, he would give the boys in my family a haircut, although we preferred to have Aunt Mary cut our hair. Although we had our own gardens, he sometimes shared produce from his gardens with our family. There were also times when he gave my mother money for our household, particularly around Christmas.

I only knew my aunt Francis for a short while. She was a fair-skinned woman of medium build who stood five foot two with black hair. She would often visit with my mother and was open to conversation. She loved to can items from their garden. She raised turtles in a little pan and would often show them to us. I do not know what she did with the turtles. I never saw them grow up. She also used to dip snuff and spit it out. I don't think Ung Green approved of this habit. She regularly attended church with my uncle. She would also drink a fruit-flavored whiskey when my uncle was not home. We used to refer to it as Sneaky Peach.

My aunt and uncle were good friends with Raymond and Ethel Harris. The Harrises lived in south end of Coeymans at the corner of Route 144 and Westerlo Street (across from Brunos) before they moved to Albany.

The Harrises would come down to church sometimes on Sunday and often stopped by to visit my aunt and uncle.

Aunt Francis had a longtime illness and passed away in her early fifties. Elsie, her youngest daughter, was a senior in high school at the time of her death. My uncle Green began to attend church in Albany. Elsie went to nursing school in Boston, and my uncle eventually moved to Albany, where he remarried.

McKinley and Mary Jones

Mary and McKinley Jones, my aunt and uncle, lived in the Bottom. I did not know my uncle very well until after he had a stroke. After the stroke he remained ill and needed assistance until his passing several years later. My uncle along with his brother Sam had a reputation for being very strict, and some people stayed clear of the Jones brothers. He was referred to by some in the Negro community as the *sheriff* of the community. It was widely said that my uncle, upon hearing that a dog had bitten his son, took the dog from the owner and slammed it to the ground, killing the dog in the process. The brothers were very close, and my uncle was said never to be the same after Sam died suddenly in his early fifties.

Aunt Mary was born Mary Magdalene Lipscomb in 1901 in Halifax, Virginia. She came to Coeymans in the 1920s before my father. She married my uncle McKinley in 1926. She was one of the founders of Riverview Missionary Baptist Church. Unlike her brother Eric, my father, she did attend church regularly. My aunt and uncle had nine children, eight girls and one boy. The youngest children, Brenda and Jennifer, were more or less my age, two years older and two years younger respectively. The other children were older, and I didn't really get to know them until I became much older. McKinley Jr., of course, became my best friend and was the best man in my wedding.

We would go with our mother to visit Aunt Mary, or sometimes Cliff, Gene, and I would go alone to get a haircut. We had two choices—either let Ung Green cut our hair or go to Aunt Mary. Ung Green seemed to be the more conservative of the two. He was a minister and did not seem to care much for style. He would simply give us a haircut like the one he had. He would cut almost all your hair off. Aunt Mary, on the other hand, would give us a brush cut that left a little pump on the top and a part on the side.

I was at an age where I didn't care much for girls. Nonetheless, when we went to Aunt Mary's house, we'd have to play with Brenda. It was a bit like torture for me. I knew that there would always be something that she would tease me about. It was a great relief when Aunt Mary would sit down and talk to us. She always seemed to have something important to tell us. Often she would share a piece of candy or cake while talking. She never raised her voice and seemed to understand everything we were saying. As I grew older, I came to appreciate her wisdom. She never presented herself as a know-it-all, but she was very much in tune with what was really happening around her, particularly in politics and world events. She made us feel important by treating whatever we had to say as if it were important. She was very patient and wise.

Mr. Brummy—The Beer Man

Mr. Brummy lived in the second house on the Hill. Alex Pointer used to live with him until he contracted tuberculosis and had to go live in a sanatorium. The house smelled like the Life Buoy soap Mr. Brummy used to bathe. His name was on the World War I war memorial in front of the old Coeymans School. I always thought his name was funny. His full name was Brummy Watkins. He was once married to a woman named Liza; however, that was before my time, and I never met her. He worked on the brickyard and loved to drink beer. In fact, I don't believe I ever saw him drink hard liquor.

Mr. Brummy would send us down to Adamo's to get his beer. He did not keep any ice in his refrigerator, so we had to go two or three times a day if he didn't go down himself. He would give us one bottle to take back. Joe would give us the five-cent deposit on the bottle. His favorite beer was Ballantine, although sometimes he would ask for Dobler, my father's preferred brand.

When Mr. Brummy went down himself, the number of bottles under his kitchen table would build up. We would peer through the window and *count the nickels*. He knew the bottles were important and would be sure to limit the number he would give us to go get his beer. There were occasions when he would give us two bottles and there were occasions when we would help ourselves to an extra bottle.

Mr. Brummy rarely cooked for himself. Rosa Logan, who lived in the Bottom would make his lunch pail. John Henry at first and then German or Clifford would take the lunch pail to him at the brickyard. He would pay for this service. I don't know why he didn't just take the lunch pail with him. He would also go to Mrs. Logan's in the evening for meals.

Voting Time

Voting was always an interesting time in Coeymans. It seems that the Negro community was virtually ignored until it came time for elections. On the night before the election, the local officials would come to Adamo's and buy rounds of drinks for the men. On the day of the elections, the officials would send cars to take them to the polls.

Everyone assumed they got paid to vote and expected to be paid. The official would show up with the car, hand out Hershey bars to the children, and give five dollars apiece to each voting adult. Mr. Teevey, who had for many years worked for the Democrats, switched his affiliation to the Republicans and continued to do the exact same thing. The irony was that with at least some of the voters, they continued to vote for the Democrats even though the Republicans were paying them and giving them a ride to the polls.

The Wedding Day Tears

I regularly went to the store for our neighbor, Miss Dicey. She would send me several times a week and pay me a dollar or so at the end of the week. On April 21, 1961, the Friday before my sister, Mary Lee's wedding to Bernard Black, I was on one of Miss Dicey's errands to the store. It was about dusk, and I had taken my bike to the store. Because we lived on the Hill, we could go fast down, but we had to walk our bikes back up. The bike did not have multiple gears. That night as I was walking my bike and nearing the top of the Hill in front of Mr. Lish's house (the first house on the Hill), I was suddenly hit from behind by a car coming up. Since I was facing traffic, the car had to have crossed the road behind me in order to hit me. I was dazed and didn't realize that I had been injured. Someone—apparently the driver of the car—was talking to me, but I don't remember what he said. When I came to, the driver was gone, and I was in the ditch on the side of the road. I could see the porch light at Ms. Dicey's house. I started to yell for help. After about five minutes, someone came out of the house and heard my pleas for help.

Soon I was surrounded by half the people on the Hill and many from down in the Bottom and Adamo's. An ambulance arrived, and that was when I realized that one of my legs had a deep gash. I was told to stay still, but everyone kept asking me questions. I don't know what I said in response to all the questions. All I do know is that I was glad to go in the ambulance. My mother rode in the ambulance with me. Other family members, including Mary Lee and Bernard, came to the hospital in a separate vehicle. Fortunately, there were no broken bones, just the gash and abrasions. The doctor had to suture the gash with wire at two levels—one inside and then another outside. At about one in the morning, I was able to go home on crutches.

The next day the family had to manage getting ready for the wedding and make sure that I was okay. The wedding was in Albany with the reception at our house in Coeymans. Some of the folks had started to celebrate before the wedding. It was one of the few times I ever heard my parents argue. My father had been drinking and started to raise his voice. My mother had been up all night with me and working all day to get the house ready for the wedding reception. She was in no mood for arguing. I found the *conversation* to be pointless and upsetting. I jumped up from the sofa where I had been sitting with one leg up, but I fell off my crutches to the floor. Nevertheless, with tears in my eyes, I yelled at my father to stop raising his voice at my mother. He looked at me, and to my and everyone else's surprise, he started to cry. I had never seen my father cry before, and I never did again.

High School—Ravena-Coeymans

I went to junior high school in the old Coeymans School building. For the first time, we were changing classrooms and getting different teachers. The two sixth grades were now one class in junior high school. We were told that we were the class of 1965. It seemed like a very long way off. I was told that junior high was going to be hard. I was determined to succeed in junior high as I had in elementary school. The course work was different, but I did make a few friends who were interested in doing well. Warren Jones, who lived north of Coeymans off Route 144, became a good friend. I also played on his father's Babe Ruth baseball team.

I also made a few friends who didn't seem interested in studying. One in particular was Donald McCool. Donald seemed to always be in trouble. One day I found a book at home that belonged to my brother German. It had a drawing of the profile of a naked girl. I took it to school and showed it to the boys, one of whom was Donald. He traced the picture and put it in his notebook. As I should have expected, Donald was caught looking at the picture in history class. Mrs. O'Neil, our teacher, had Donald on her list of people to keep an eye on. Before she could retrieve the picture, he tore it up into many pieces. Not to be deterred, Mrs. O'Neil made him sit in front of her until she put it back together with tape. She then marched him down to Mr. Rooney, the school principal. There he told them that he had gotten the picture from me. Mrs. O'Neil couldn't believe it. I was one of her best students. She called me to the office. I told her that I had brought the book to school, but I did not copy it. Mr. Rooney asked us both to remain in detention after school. He gave both of us a whack across our butts three times with a wooden two-by-four board inscribed with the words "Board of Education." It really hurt, but we wouldn't cry.

The following year Donald and some friends threw eggs at Mrs. O'Neil's car on Halloween. Dried egg yolks are very difficult to remove. Mrs. O'Neil's husband was physically unable to clean the car. As soon as we came to class, Mrs. O'Neil, red as a beet, grabbed Donald by the ear and dragged him to the front of the room. She told him how detestable he was in her mind. We all felt sorry for her. She then took Donald to the principal's office, where he was again asked to remain for detention. I believe the Board of Education was applied once again.

I went to high school at the Ravena high school building. Those were difficult days. I was now a young man and needed things my parents could not afford. I was as athletic as any of the other kids. My problem was that I did not have any gym clothes or sneakers. I went the whole ninth-grade year playing gym in my school clothes. Indoors, I played in my socks. I could not play basketball because the other kids would step on my feet. Some days I would stay home from school on gym days. While the coach never said anything to me, I later learned that he had mentioned to the other coaches that I didn't want to change clothes in gym. I don't know which hurt more, the truth or the lie.

Despite my problems with gym, I continued to do well in all my classes. I even got a B in gym—a grade that had more to do with my dress than it did with my ability. In the end, it was good to know that as I entered tenth grade, I would be taking New York State Regents courses that would help me get into college. This was unusual for Negroes. They were usually put on an industrial arts or business track that didn't lead to college. This would help them get trade school jobs when they graduated. I was determined to go to college, even though I had no idea how I would get the money to go.

The next year the new high school opened on Route 9W north of Ravena. It was a beautiful school, and everything was state of the art. The gym facilities were second to none. I loved the place. For the first time, using money from my odd jobs, I was able to dress for gym and wear new sneakers. I tried out for junior varsity basketball, but I did not make the team. Nonetheless, I put together a team that played scrimmages with the ninth grade down at the old Coeymans School gym. Mr. Traver, who had been one of my earlier coaches, invited us to play his team as practice for their regular games. When we weren't playing, I'd referee the intramural squad with Mr. Doyle, another teacher.

A Room of My Own

After my uncle Green moved to Albany, I don't recall whether my father asked for the right to move into my uncle's flat on the second floor of our house or we just did it. Our first problem was that there was no interior staircase. No one seemed to be interested in occupying the second floor other than Gene, Cliff, and me. As we surveyed the situation, we noticed that there used to be an interior staircase that had been removed some years before. At first, we just pulled the boards up and built a ladder in the hallway to the upstairs hallway. I immediately moved into what was my uncle's living room, and Gene and Cliff moved into the former dining room.

I liked my room a lot. It was the first time I had a room to myself—a big improvement over sleeping with four people in one bed. We didn't turn the power on upstairs, so we used kerosene lanterns at night. Since there was no heat upstairs, we cut a hole in the ceiling downstairs above the potbelly stove to warm the bedrooms upstairs. We had to leave the bedroom doors open so the heat could come in.

When lying in my bed and looking out the window at night, I could see the driveway of the house formerly occupied by Ernest and Sylvester Ray. Mr. Ray had drowned in Coeymans Creek in April 1958, and George and Mildred Sims now lived in the house. There were large white Calistoga wagon wheels on each side of the driveway. I could see the snowdrift upon the wheels. I knew that eventually much of the wheels would be covered in drifting snow. It was great having my own room with my own stuff.

The Hill was in transition, and people began to move. There were whispers that the houses might be torn down and replaced, but no one seemed to pay much attention to the rumors. Mr. Brummy retired from the brickyard and moved to Albany. Because I had been in his house many times, I knew it well. No one seemed to be moving into the house. One day I took a crowbar and hammer over to the house and removed the staircase. Although it was quite heavy, with several stops along the way, I managed to drag the staircase over to our house and altered it to fit in our hallway. We now had staircase access to the second floor. Pearl then moved upstairs to Elsie's former bedroom, and we had the power turned on.

I went with my mother to a secondhand store in Ravena. I saw a small black-and-white television in a beautiful wood cabinet. The television did not work. My mother bought it for me for twelve dollars. She knew that although I was only fourteen years old, from my days working with Tommy Wilson, I could fix the television. I took it upstairs as soon as we got home. I began to work on the television. Not long thereafter, I had it working. It could only get one channel! No matter. This was my television!

Soon my world seemed as if it came to an end. The local paper reported that a plan had been announced to tear down all the houses on the Hill and in the Bottom and build new ones for those families who could afford them. We later found out that the brickyard had been sold. The town of Coeymans had apparently determined that the Negro community at the north end of Coeymans was an eyesore. The owners of the property had decided to remove the homes and the people. There was never any discussion between the owners of the property and the Negro community. People heard bits of information from gossip circles and little else. At one point, there was an article in the newspaper about housing being built, but nothing actually happened. There was, however, a rush by families to find other housing in Coeymans without talking to their neighbors. Many families seemed to do so overnight. No one offered to help us find other housing. We knew that we would have to move to Albany.

WHERE THERE'S A WILL, THERE'S A WAY
1962–66

Coeymans to Albany

Mary Lee, married and living on North Pearl Street near Livingston Avenue, helped us find a place to live in Albany not too far from her apartment. William Mays, a tailor, owned a house at 744 Broadway. He wanted eighty dollars a month in rent—an amount almost nine times that which my parents were paying for the flat in Coeymans. The house was at the corner of Broadway and Wilson Streets with Broadway being a main thoroughfare in and out of Albany to the adjacent cities of Menands, Watervliet, and Troy to the north. It was an old turn-of-the-century building with three floors (walk-up) and a basement. Mr. Mays used the basement for his tailor shop. The building was a residence from an earlier age with large rooms on each floor. As such, the entry had a grand hallway that led to a flight of stairs that ascended another two levels. The entire hallway from the first floor to the third floor was open and presented a real challenge for heating. We kept the doors off the hallways closed at all times.

We were one of the last families in Coeymans to move. Some of the houses in the Bottom and on the Hill had already been demolished. At that time, eight of the children and four grandchildren were still part of our household. On moving day I remained in Albany to help put things in place as the truck delivered our belongings. This time I did have my own room, albeit a very small one at the end of the hall on the second floor. As I was putting things away, I heard a loud noise as if something had fallen in the house. When I looked, I did not find anything that had fallen or looked disturbed. I forgot about the incident until the next truckload arrived. After we emptied the truck on the last trip, I asked if they had forgotten my television. There were some snickering and sheepish smiles before someone yelled, "Daddy dropped your television out of the window. It ain't no good now." The snickering turned to laughter. I was devastated and wanted to cry, but I was determined not to give anyone that satisfaction. My mother bought me that television, and I had repaired it. She looked at me and knew that it meant a lot to me. She was not laughing. It was the one thing I had that I felt was truly my own. Now it was lost forever.

After we settled in, I took on the job of painting. I painted every room in the house. Mr. Mays supplied the paint. I also built an apron around the kitchen sink so that my mother would have a countertop to place dishes on. I then took on the monumental task of plastering the wall in the main hallway. The plaster had fallen down from the top of the second floor all the way down to the bottom of the first. I didn't know anything about plastering, but I was determined to repair the wall. It was very unsightly. I used so many bags of plaster that Mr. Mays told me that he was not going to buy anymore, but I finally did get it plastered. It was not pretty, but it was a 100 percent improvement. Afterward, I painted the hallway a two-toned color—dark brown on the bottom and off-white on the top. It looked really sharp. Mr. Mays was surprised at how well the hallway turned out. I then prayed that he would not raise the rent because of the improvement.

Making New Friends

The move to Albany, just thirteen miles away, also marked the end of my close friendship with my childhood friends Jimmy Gladney, Tony Kittle, Perry Comithier, and Billy Stevens. Yes, we kept in touch; however, time had its way, and our closeness became more of a memory and less of a reality. We began to go our separate ways.

We didn't know many people in Albany. Our cousin Lenzy and his wife, Margaret, lived on North Pearl Street diagonally across from our house. John Henry lived two blocks up North Pearl Street, and Mary Lee lived another two blocks up from John. We didn't know a lot about the streets in Albany. Every day was a little adventure to explore the neighborhood. Bobby and Tony Wilson came by to visit us, and we began to hang around with them from time to time. I soon met some guys around the neighborhood as well. I used to go up to Mary Lee's house a lot, and on the way I met new people—Sam West, Rickey Jenkins, Robert "Red" Conners, Joe Thornton, the Surgicks, and many others. At one time or another, we all played basketball on the city basketball courts in back of the Albany Nursing Home directly opposite where we lived. Sometimes some of us would just walk around the city from the south end to the north end. There were different groups of teenagers who seemed to hang out in the different neighborhoods.

Red Conners and I used to hang out a lot in the beginning. It soon became clear to Red that he and I were really different people. He was more interested in *getting over* on people by any means, and I was just trying to get to know people. Red soon realized this and began to respect the fact that I was not going to join him in getting into trouble.

Although he talked a good game, he never asked me to do anything that was wrong. Nonetheless, Red soon found himself in and out of jail, and we drifted apart. Sam, on the other hand, was always quiet. Our best times were spent not playing sports but looking for parties and girls. We would spend hours on end on the front steps of houses, talking to the girls through the window or out on the porch. From time to time, Joe Thornton or Bobby Wilson would join us. None of us took any of this seriously, although at times we all felt our hormones kicking in.

High School—Albany

I began high school at Albany High School in the middle of the fall of my sophomore year. Fortunately, I did not have to go to the Annex. In Albany, the students were put on a track for college or trades. The students who were not on a college track were automatically sent to the Albany High Annex.

Norman McConney was one of the first students I met in school. He had heard that we would be coming to Albany High. He came over to me and introduced himself and began to fill me in on things. We immediately became friends and have remained such over the years even though we hardly ever see each other. I soon met other students, including many in higher grades and those down at the Annex. Of all the people, Norman and I seemed to get along the best. We were in a lot of the same classes. Norman was determined to excel in all his classes, and I was focused on mine. We dressed different than most other students in that we always seemed to have a jacket or sweater and tie on and carried a briefcase. Although we were different, we nonetheless hung around with a lot of the *brothers and sisters*. In a way, they were proud that at least some of our people were looking to achieve some level of success. We never saw ourselves as better than everyone else. We were simply in the *struggle*, trying to do the best we knew how.

Although I went to work right after school every day and all day on Saturdays, I still took college entrance courses. I wanted to be an architect. I didn't know much about architecture schools, but I knew I needed to know math. I loved math and was pretty good with all math courses. At Albany High, Norman McConney and I were in the same trigonometry class. Norman struggled all year, and I tried to help him as much as I could. However, when it came time for the final exam, I misread several questions and used the wrong formulas. Norman passed the exam, and I failed! I was devastated. I used the money I earned from work to pay to go to summer school to make up the course and to qualify for the calculus course the next year.

I was a fast runner. I was going to try out for track with my brother Eugene in the spring. I even spoke to Coach Becker about doing so. Then one day Eugene asked me if I took showers after gym class. I was totally miffed by the question. For me it was never any question about taking a shower. Gene told me that Coach Becker had heard from the coach in Ravena that I was reluctant to take showers! Then it dawned on me that my past gym classes in the ninth grade had come back to haunt me. I was angry at both coaches. I didn't see either as being fair. Coach Becker only needed to ask my current gym teacher, who was a stickler about everyone showering before returning to class. I decided then and there that I would never play any sport for that coach. I did not try out for track or any other sport.

The Parties

We were not yet old enough to go to bars or buy alcohol. On weekends and sometimes during the week (in the summer), we would go to house parties or parties at the Trinity Center, the local teen center on the south end of Albany. All the Negro kids from Albany High School and Scyhuler High School (there were two high schools at that time) would go to these parties. The popular tunes of the day were "Duke of Earl" by Gene Chandler, the "Twist" by Chubby Checker, "What'd I Say" by Ray Charles, "Your Precious Love" by Jerry Butler, "Lost Someone" by James Brown, and "Saturday Night" by Sam Cooke, to name a few. We preferred the slow songs, such as "I'm So Proud" by the Impressions (Curtis Mayfield as lead singer), "Pain in My Heart" by Otis Redding, and "You'll Want Me Back" by Major Lance.

These parties would sometimes start spontaneously with a few people gathering together. Soon we'd put a red bulb in the socket and turn on the music. People walking the neighborhood would stop by and start dancing. The parties usually started after ten at night and would sometimes last to one in the morning or so. Unfortunately, things did not always go smoothly. Sometimes people would bring cheap wine or liquor to the party or go out and get some. There seemed to always be a few people who would use bully tactics and end up in a fight of some kind. This usually stopped at pushing and shoving, but there were times when things got really violent with someone getting beat up pretty bad or even stabbed. Our exit strategy was to get a girl and go sit on a stoop away from the disturbance. I never liked to see fighting and certainly not stabbings or shootings.

There were a few people who had a reputation for being bad. They seem to look forward to the opportunity to beat someone up and then wait for the news to pass through the neighborhood the next day. Each time the story was told, it seemed to enhance the reputation of the bad actor. When I lived in Coeymans, I used to hear about Hiawatha White and Leon Wilson getting into fights with people. Once we moved to Albany, the days of Hiawatha and Leon seemed to have passed, and there was a new cast of characters on the scene. One was Bucky Greenwood, who used to train at boxing at Trinity Community Center. He would not hesitate to employ his skills on the streets of Albany. He was not a big man. He was about five foot seven and weighed about 150 pounds. Nevertheless, it seemed like he was always looking for people to fight. Although he beat up most of his unskilled opponents, sometimes he would meet his match even though they lacked his skills. I can recall his taking on Charles "Tinker" Leigh, an All-American high school football and basketball player at Albany High School, who became a professional football player with the Baltimore Colts and later with the Miami Dolphins. Bucky initiated the conversation, and a lot of trash-talking took place before the fight. It was clear that Bucky wanted to fight and Tinker did not. I can only guess that Bucky was thinking that if he could beat such a star, it would enhance his reputation. Why he thought he could beat Tinker is another question. Perhaps because they both had been drinking, Bucky saw it as an opportunity. He could not have been more wrong. Tinker kicked his butt in front of a crowd, which had grown as the word spread about the imminent fight. It was not Bucky's last fight or his last butt kicking.

Young Life

I first went to the Neighborhood House on North Pearl Street with Sam and Red. The Neighborhood House, on the north end of the city where I lived, was much like Trinity Community Center on the south end of the city. It was a gathering place for youth. We met Fred Aldorfer at the Neighborhood House. Fred was a boyish-looking white adult, perhaps twenty-five years old or so, who wanted to talk to us about getting involved in various activities at the Neighborhood House. Since other people were gathering there, we'd come by and listen. Fred gave all the guys a plain English New Testament Bible and asked us to join him in discussing the modern-day translations. For the first time in many years, my Sunday school teaching was coming back alive. We were all familiar with the King James Version of the Bible, but this was the first time we ever saw a modern translation of the New Testament.

Fred was clearly not from the neighborhood. We would often laugh at some of his expressions. To him they were natural, but to us they sounded quite *white*. Fred could play a little basketball, although Joe Thornton would usually run circles around him. We liked Fred because at least he tried to fit in while at the same time we knew he had an agenda—to lead us to a Christian lifestyle. Fred lived in the projects on the south end of town with his wife and little boy. He was married to a Negro woman. While that was not typical of Albany, the Negroes in the community didn't seem to mind.

We gathered for Bible study every Friday at the Neighborhood house. Fred began each meeting with prayer and asked us to read different passages from the Bible. We often joked about who could read and who could not. Sometimes the discussion led to personal testimony by someone in the group, but there was no pressure for anyone to say anything. We also discussed things going on in the community and offered our opinions on them. It was one of those rare occasions where it seemed someone cared about what you thought.

The Young Life Bible was the beginning of my adult walk in Christianity. Yes, Fred, wherever you are today, the seeds that were sown so long ago did indeed take hold and are bearing fruit today.

Kennedy Assassination

I was in my sophomore year on that fateful day in November 1963. I recall sitting in social studies class when our teacher, Mrs. Jacobs, told us what had happened. We were all numb. We didn't know what to say or do. Kennedy was the only president of the United States we knew. I gave no thought to conspiracy, and I didn't even think that our country may be in danger. I could only think about Abraham Lincoln. We had read about his assassination. He, too, had been shot in the head. We did not go home early. Mrs. Jacobs just talked to us. When we were let go at the usual time, we ran home. It was the only thing on television. The black and white pictures were played over and over again on television.

In the days following the assassination, particularly after Oswald was killed by Ruby, there was speculation about who was really responsible. However, in the Negro community, there was a deep sense of loss. The Kennedy we knew was a good man who stood up for the civil rights of Negroes. Johnson had a reputation for doing just the opposite. He was a southerner from Texas. School days were not the same. Somehow, we automatically came of age. After all, this assassination came only a few months after the March on Washington, where a quarter of a million people stood in protest at the steps of the Lincoln Memorial. I was more determined now to go to college.

The Goldsteins

In high school I largely supported myself. My father's health was failing, and he soon retired from work. He had a small pension from his job and his social security. Given the cost of rent and utility bills in Albany together with all the children and grandchildren staying in the household, everyone needed to chip in to help support the family. Mary Lee was a seamstress Decorators' Workroom, a custom drapery and upholstery shop on Central Avenue in Colonie. When we moved to Albany, it became uneconomical for me to take the bus to Coeymans to work for Mrs. Adamo. Mary Lee got me a job cleaning up at Decorators' Workroom. It was a family business owned by Nat and Evelyn Goldstein. Evelyn's sister Lillian and nephew Mort (Lillian's son) were also owners. Although the Goldsteins had two sons (Leonard and Steve), neither of them was in the business at the time I worked for the Goldsteins.

Essentially, the business served as the workroom for interior decorators. The major furniture and department stores would sell custom drapery, slipcovers, and upholstery to customers, and the workroom would produce the product. Although the customers did not know it, the same people worked on their order whether they ordered from the department stores or the finer furniture stores. Since most of the materials used to make the items came from the same manufacturer, the main difference between the items the customers received was in the price the customers paid.

The business employed eight to ten people who worked on the clock or by piecemeal (per item produced). The women did all the sewing except that Nat would sometimes sew the upholstery when he did not want to wait for a seamstress. The men would go out to the homes of customers to measure for and install the drapery and slipcovers. The upholstery orders would be brought into the shop. Evelyn and Lillian handled the business end, although Lillian did help with the drapery. Nat was the *boss* for cutting all material and upholstery work. He trained all the men who worked for him. When I arrived, Nat was no longer going out on jobs except in the case of emergency or when there was a particularly difficult job. He was very good at what he did.

Although I was hired to cleanup, Nat soon had me cutting the material for drapery and slipcovers. He even bought me a pair of left-handed scissors. I learned not only how to measure the cuts but also how to cut with the bias in the cloth. He also taught me how to cut welting and pleating for slipcovers. I learned the shortcuts of doing several jobs at the same time. He later purchased me an electric scissors, which was a great relief for my hands. Nat and I became pretty good friends—he as teacher and me as student. He soon taught me how to cut slipcovers and do upholstery. Every now and then, he would take me out on jobs to give on-site training in the homes of customers. It did not take me long to learn.

Once I got my driver's license, my job expanded to delivering the slipcovers. I would use the company car or truck to travel all over the Albany-Troy-Schenectady region to deliver the slipcovers. From time to time, Evelyn would ask me to do a slipcover cutting job. I never did get to the level of working piecemeal as did the other men who got paid based on the type of slipcover cutting or drapery installation. I was only part-time after school and Saturdays. I started to get increases in salary as my skills increased, and I was soon making $1.50 per hour. I recall the time when I was able to save up to $40.00 and bought my mother a blue coat for Christmas. She had often commented that she never had a new coat in her life. When she saw the coat, she slumped into the nearby chair and cried with joy. I too could not hold back the tears.

75 North Swan Street

We seemed to move every year or so in Albany. We lived at 744 Broadway, 157 Colonie Street, 31 Clinton Avenue, 437 Clinton Avenue, North Pearl Street, and 51 Livingston Avenue. We moved from Livingston Avenue up to 75 North Swan Street. The house had two rooms on the first floor, three rooms on the second floor, and an unfinished basement. My mother and father, four sisters, one grandchild, and I moved into the house.

There was only one bathroom in the house, and it was in a corner of the kitchen. It was an area that tightly enclosed the sink, the shower stall and commode. The space limitations required that you back into the bathroom. The kitchen had a sink, stove, refrigerator and hot water heater. There was room behind the hot water heater that could be used for a bedroom. I partitioned the area with studs and covered them with cardboard from grocery boxes in lieu of sheetrock. The space became my parents' bedroom.

I slept in the closet space underneath the staircase. Because of the size of the space, I backed into my bed in the closet each night and pulled the door shut. Under the circumstances, I probably had the best room in the house. Eventually, I cleaned out the basement and partitioned off a portion of it with cardboard to make my bedroom. It also served as my private space where I could get away to do my homework. I painted one of the foundation walls and wrote a poem in calligraphy on it. Although we did not have a telephone in the house, I tapped into a telephone line attached to the house so I could make calls. I removed the bells from the telephone so no one would hear it ring. I did not know the telephone number. Somehow the telephone company never detected my telephone. The winter was particularly cold because there was no heat in the basement and the area was often damp. Nevertheless, I had my space—alone.

Swan Street was a busy street on Arbor Hill. We lived across the street from Saint Joseph's High School—a Catholic school now largely attended by Negro children. Going west on Swan Street, there was Ms. Catherine's restaurant and Kittles, a nightclub where Miss Maggie's Children played soul music on weekends. Henry Dargan, who was from Selkirk, New York (about three miles north of Coeymans), and also a graduate of Ravena High School and Howard University, operated a pharmacy. Henry also had his own airplane that he often flew to various parts of the country. At the end of the busy part of the street on the corner of Livingston Avenue, there was the McNeil Barber Shop, where I now went to get my haircut. McNeil was arguably the best Negro barber in the city. He and his associates kept up with all the latest styles.

It was on North Swan Street that I had my first encounter with the police in Albany. Sam West and I had just left my house and walked west on Swan Street toward First Street. It was the Fourth of July weekend, and it seemed that everyone was out and about. We stopped at the corner, and Jasper came over to offer some firecrackers. "Let's see what you got, man," I said to Jasper. He reached in his pocket and pulled out some firecrackers and a couple of cherry bombs (large firecrackers). "We don't want no cherry bombs. Just give us some firecrackers." "That'll be three bills for six," said Jasper.

"C'om on, man. This is me," said Sam. "You can do better than that."

"All right, Sam. Two dollars, but you owe me, man," said Jasper.

As soon as Jasper handed over the firecrackers, three to each of us, a police car rolled up, and a patrolman got out and went to the telephone booth on the corner. This was not uncommon, and it happened fairly frequently when the officers wanted to make personal calls. Jasper looked at the policeman in the telephone booth and said, "Watch me scare the shit out of him."

"Man, are you out of your mind?" I said. "He is going to be pissed, and everyone is going to jail."

"No way," said Jasper. "He got to know who did it."

"I am out of here," Sam and I said almost simultaneously. We had seen the cops in action, and they would beat the hell out of you for just looking like you did something wrong. We turned to walk east on North Swan Street when we heard what had to be a cherry bomb.

As we turned around to look, the cop looked right at Sam and me. "Hold it right there, you motherfuckers," he said. We froze. He called on his radio for assistance and then told us to get against the wall. I could only think of the firecrackers in our pockets. I said to Sam as quietly as I could, "Put them in the palm of your hand so he won't find them on you."

There we stood with our hands pressed against the wall with the firecrackers under them. Within minutes there were a half of a dozen police cars at the intersection and fanning out as the crowd continued to grow. I yelled, "Jasper, you'd better tell them what you did, man. We're not going to jail for you."

Jasper, who had gone inside his house, came out and said, "Officer, I did it. They didn't have anything to do with it."

The officer shoved him against the wall next to us. All of us were frisked while leaning against the wall. The officer found firecrackers on Jasper, but not on Sam or me. "Turn around," said the officer. "You two," he said, pointing at Sam and me, "get the fuck out of here." Sam and I walked slowly east away from the scene. When we got to my house, we ran into the basement. Jasper was taken downtown to the police station, where he was reportedly asked to implicate Sam and me in exchange for his release. Apparently, Jasper did not acquiesce, and we were not arrested.

That Regrettable Fight

I got to be fairly well known around school and around the neighborhoods. Although somewhat short, I was reasonably well built and strong. I sometimes wore a beret, a derby, or a panama hat. Whenever I wore the panama hat, I would be mistaken for Fred Lee from a distance. Fred was well known in the neighborhood as being a tough young man. I knew Fred and never had any problems with him. I was always concerned that someone who didn't like Fred might mistake me for him. Although it happened often, fortunately, they soon realized that I was not Fred. On the other hand, I found myself in a fight from an unlikely source.

Eddie Lewis was a good friend of my brother Eugene. They ran track in high school. Eddie was a great guy to know. We got along well. Eugene and I would often walk to school with him and sometimes hang out at his house. His mom was also very pleasant and always treated us well. Eddie had two brothers, Ray and Earl, and a sister named Gwen, who was in my class. Ray and Earl were a couple of years younger than me. During the summer it was very common to play basketball down at the playground on North Pearl Street. Earl was a good player but not as good as Eddie, and like all of us, he was certainly not destined for stardom. I thought Earl was a pretty good friend until one day at the playground, he was determined to start a fight. I was very surprised because it was so out of character, and fighting the brother of a good friend was not something I wanted to do. I told him that I did not want to fight him and preferred to leave. I walked up to the corner of North Pearl and Wilson Streets, and Earl and his friends followed me. With the agitation of his friends, he continued to insist on what he was going to do to me. Finally, he said something that set me off, and I hit him at least a dozen times before he knew what happened. All he could do was to try to tie me up. Some older men pulled us apart. I knew I hurt him. I could see it in his face as he began to choke up. I told him that we could finish up on the Hill (Arbor Hill) if he wanted to continue. He did not. I felt bad not for Earl but for Eddie. He was my friend, and I shouldn't have been fighting with his brother.

I later found out that the reason for the fight was because some of Earl's friends had been talking about whether anyone could beat me. Somehow, merely because of the way I looked, I became the target. Earl was going to show his friends that he could beat me up. Earl's brother Ray and Mike, my sister Carol's boyfriend, were following in the footsteps of Bucky Greenwood. They were getting a reputation among their peers as being bad. I ran into Ray and Mike on the Hill, and they stood at opposite sides of me as if they were ready to take me on. Mike said, "I heard you took on Earl?"

I said, "No, I believe it's the other way around. I don't know where it all came from. All I know was that Earl started selling *wolf tickets* in front of his friends. We got into it, and he got hurt. I told him that if he wanted to continue, he could see me on the Hill. I haven't seen him."

Ray said, "Was this thing on, or was it over?"

I said, "I don't know. I didn't start it. I am not looking for Earl. I told him that I didn't want to fight him."

Mike said, "So it's over as far as you are concerned?"

I said, "Yeah, it's over for me unless he come messing with me." They looked at each other and then at me. Then they walked on down the Hill. I later saw Eddie walking to school on the other side of the street. I yelled, "Hello!" from a distance, and he waved back. I don't recall seeing or speaking to Eddie since that time.

Malcom X

"They finally got him," I heard someone say from the living room upstairs.

"Got who?" I said from my room in the basement.

"Somebody shot Malcom X in New York. He was one of d'em black Muslim who hate white people," came the reply. I knew who Malcom X was, but I did not know much about him. I recalled him saying about the assassination of John F. Kennedy that the "chickens came home to roost," implying that perhaps the president had been involved in similar activity. Not everyone involved in the civil rights movement embraced the talk of the younger black people. Despite the treatment of Negroes in the South, the older people still preferred nonviolence and rejected racism by anyone, including other Negroes.

While spending time in jail, Malcom converted to the Muslim religion and joined the Nation of Islam led by Elijah Muhammad. He became the radical voice of the Nation of Islam and engendered the disdain of civil rights leaders and older Negroes who were not accustomed to Malcom's assertions of self-determination and defense. After a period of travel in Africa and the Middle East, which included completing the Hajj (an annual Islamic pilgrimage to Mecca after which he was given the honorific title of El-Hajj), Malcom repudiated the Nation of Islam, disavowed racism, and founded Muslim Mosque, Inc. and the Organization of Afro-American Unity. He continued to emphasize Pan-Africanism, black self-determination, and black self-defense. Now February 21, 1965, it was reported that Malcom X, at the age of thirty-nine, had been assassinated at the Audubon Ballroom in New York City, reportedly by members of the Nation of Islam.

I ran upstairs to see the news on television. The media was speculating about not only who shot Malcom but also why. The mayor of New York was asking for people to remain calm out of concern about possible rioting and retaliation. For me, this was very much like the assassination of President Kennedy—except the white people seemed to think Malcom got what was coming to him and the black people were in mourning for the loss of a leader. At eighteen years of age, I did not know what to think. It was years later before I fully understood the role of Malcom X in the civil rights movement and the lives of black people in America.

The Role—Fact or Fiction

Senior Class Officers

Although I did not play sports or attend many school events in high school because of my work schedule, I did make many new friends in my various classes. I think I was regarded as somewhat of a nerd and a loner to those who did not know me. I always carried a briefcase full of stuff. I studied at school because I did not have the time to study at work or a place to study at home. Given my profile, no one could have been more surprised than me to learn that my class had elected me to be the senior class treasurer.

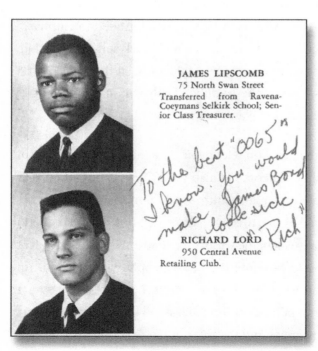

JAMES LIPSCOMB
75 North Swan Street
Transferred from Ravena-Coeymans Selkirk School; Senior Class Treasurer.

To the best "0065" I know. You would make James Bond look sick. Rich

RICHARD LORD
950 Central Avenue
Retailing Club.

My high school days can be best summed up by my role in the senior high school play. Next to the senior prom, the play was the event of the senior year. I never went to the prom in the eleventh or twelfth grade. I didn't have the money for a prom event, and if I did, the girl I wanted to take was already going with someone else. The play, however, merely required me to play a part. I played the part of the popular movie character James Bond. I was 0065. The evening was going very well with several individual performances preceding the play. My job as James Bond was to find the class Will that had been purloined. I got to wear a suit and tie (not out of character for me) for the part. In my search for the Will, I encountered some tough guys. I soon discovered that Mr. Lincoln, the school principal, had stolen the Will. This discovery caused quite a stir in the audience. I finally fought the tough guys and recovered the Will. I exited the stage with a James Bond type line by saying, "Where there's a will, there's a way." This line aptly sums up my determination in high school to succeed.

College Bound

Although the play was the highlight of my senior year in high school, I did have my share of disappointments. My brother Clifford had transferred from Cobleskill Community College to Howard University in 1964 as a junior, the same year Eugene began as a freshman at Howard. I wanted to be an architect, so I applied to Endicott-Johnson Community College and the State University of New York at Stony Brook. Jay Wyche, my brother German's brother-in-law, drove me out to the Stony Brook for an interview. We had no idea that it was so far from New York City, let alone from Albany. The trip took the entire day. In the end, the dean of admissions advised me that I was not going to be accepted. I was also rejected at Endicott-Johnson. My whole world had caved in. I had taken college courses and done reasonably well on my regents exams. Yet I was rejected!

Fortunately, my guidance counselor at Albany High School knew the dean of admissions at Hudson Valley Community College in Troy, New York. I applied and was accepted. Norman McConney had also been accepted. It was a two-year school without dormitory facilities. It was expected that all students would commute. Norman and I decided to get our own apartment in Albany. We rented the back apartment on the first floor at 103 North Lark Street in Albany.

The day of my move was quite emotional. I was at once excited about finally being able to live on my own and at the same time lamenting the fact that I would be leaving my mother alone to deal with so many problems, including those with her and my father's failing health. I packed my footlocker and dragged it out of the basement to the sidewalk. I then walked into the house and said goodbye as if I was going a thousand miles away rather than simply up the street a few blocks. I embraced my mother and held back the tears. Little did she know how much I wanted to cry, but I didn't want her or anyone else to see me crying. Little did I know until much later how hard it was on her. I was told that she cried the rest of the day.

I didn't know how I was going to get out to Hudson Valley every day since I did not have a car. I would have to take the bus. Norman and I started out commuting by bus, but we soon met some friends who lived around Albany and who agreed to give us a ride. Sean McGee, who lived in Albany, was the first to offer me a ride.

Once on campus, I soon discovered several people from Albany attending the college. Janice Woodard, Frank Lownes, and Rick Lownes among others were all attending. I was in a liberal arts curriculum. I had given up on pursuing a career in architecture. I found the courses fairly easy, studied when I needed to, and generally did very well on all my exams. The dean would come through the lounge from time to time and break up the card games. He thought bridge had a redeeming value, but poker and tonk did not, particularly when there was money involved.

My cousin John Frank, a patrolman at the Albany Police Department, helped me buy my first car, a 1956 DeSoto. I paid $125 for the car. It had a leak in the transmission, so I had to drive with a case of transmission oil in the trunk to fill up the car on a regular basis. I was able to continue to work for the Goldsteins. When work was slow in the summer, Evelyn would nonetheless have me come in and work off the books. She didn't have to do this, but she knew I needed the money. Nat Goldstein took me to Armory Garage in Albany on Central Avenue at Colvin, where I bought a 1959 Chevrolet Impala for $600. Since I did not have any credit, my brother John co-signed for the car. I paid my payments out of the money I made working for the Goldsteins.

I did make a lot of new friends at Hudson Valley. Nick Kaiser became a good friend. He played in a local band and pledged a fraternity. I kept in touch with him after I went to Howard. I still recall his very moving letter to me at the time of the assassination of Martin Luther King. He was genuine in his feeling of loss. It served to remind me at that time, the time of *black power*, that good character and behavior did not have a color. There were a number of other buddies who got together at the beer garden across the road from the campus, sat around in the cars in the parking lot between classes or at lunch, or just hung out in the lounge to play cards. The friends at Hudson Valley were local people who lived at or near home.

After my first year at Hudson Valley, Norman decided to move in with his girlfriend, and I had to return home because although I was working for the Goldsteins part-time, I could not afford the rent by myself. By that time, my parents had moved once again. This time they moved to 437 Clinton Avenue in Albany.

On weekends I led a different life. I hung around with my friends in Albany—Sam West and Bobby Wilson. Sam and Bobby had become my running buddies. Later Billy Stevens's cousin, Harry Stevens, joined our group. Harry was known as the *banker* because he had a job at a bank downtown and always seemed to be dressed up. He actually liked playing the role. Sometimes he would put dollar bills in his pockets and pant cuffs, and at opportune moments he'd retrieve them with flair. We, of course, allowed him to continue in that role to the point of paying the tab for the group. None of them had a license or a car at the time. I provided the transportation. We would go everywhere around town and out of town. We drove to Washington, DC, to visit Cliff and Gene at Howard University once. Unfortunately, I had to do all the driving while they slept. We stopped in Newark to get a room and I had barely closed my eyes when the three of them said they were not sleepy and wanted to continue on to DC. As soon as we got on the New Jersey Turnpike again, all three were asleep!

Our favorite hangout was Kittles, the bar on North Swan Street. It was the place to be seen and to hear the best R & B. The band Miss Maggie's Children would play all the latest songs—"The Price," "Pain in My Heart," "Cool Jerk," "Walking the Dog," "Mr. Pitiful," "Papa's Got a Brand-New Bag," and "My Girl." We would leave Kittles in time to catch Miss Catherine or Chef Woody to get something to eat before closing time. Miss Catherine operated a restaurant next door to Kittles. Catherine was well known in the community for her chitlins and potato salad. We would visit her sometimes before going to Kittles.

Chef Woody was an older man who worked in a bar on Broadway called Two Sisters. Chef had a reputation for making the best fried chicken in Albany. He was also forgetful. He loved the ladies, and they doted on him; however, he showed disdain for the men. He seemed insecure around men. Chef, a short man about five foot four, had a rather elongated head and a clubfoot. The chef's cap on his head tilted to one side further exaggerated his appearance.

Sam and I walked into Two Sisters and went straight to the back where the kitchen was located. The smell of fried chicken was already in the air in the bar and provided a trail as we went toward the kitchen. We were in luck. No one was ahead of us. "Good evening, Chef," I said on my approach to the counter. Chef just looked up as if he did not care about the greeting. "Can we get a couple of chicken dinners?" I said in a rather strong voice to show my maturity.

"What you want on it?" Chef responded.

"Put some salt and pepper on them. Add a little cayenne too." Chef started preparing the chicken and was about to dip the chicken in flour when two ladies came up behind us.

"Hey, Woody," one of them yelled. "Give me some sugar." She leaned over to give him a kiss. "You doing chicken tonight?" she asked.

"I do chicken every night. What you won't?"

"Just a couple of dinners. We are soooo hungry. We came over here from Dorsey's to give you some sugar and get some chicken."

Chef looked at her in a lustful way and smiled. "I got a couple going right now," he said.

"Whoa, Chef! Those are Sam and my dinners," I said.

Chef looked at me with a glare and said, "They ain't yours unless I give 'em to you."

Now I was getting pissed off. "We placed our order before anyone else showed up."

Chef picked up the frying pan from the stove where he was heating the grease. "You'd better get the hell outa here. Don't tell me how to run my business," he said with a knife-cutting glare. With smiles from ear to ear, the ladies stepped back from the counter to clear a path for Chef to throw the grease. Sam grabbed me by the shoulders and pulled me backward until we were out of range of the grease. That was the last time I went to Two Sisters and the last time I saw Chef.

Sometimes we'd go down to Coeymans to the former Adamo's—now called George's after the man who rented the place from Mr. Adamo. George Henry Lipscomb Jr. (no relation) completely renovated the bar and made it a contemporary place for adults to spend an evening. A number of people would come down from Albany, particularly in the summer. He did not have live entertainment, but he did have a jukebox with all the latest hits. He did permit dancing. It was a place for a lot of old friends in Coeymans and Albany to get together.

In anticipation of my graduation from Hudson Valley, I applied to Howard University as a transfer student. I was accepted and given a limited scholarship. This meant that I was leaving Albany for the first time. I was also leaving friends, including Bobby, Harry, and Sam. I did not appreciate it at the time, but I was also leaving Coeymans and Albany for a life that would change my worldview forever.

SAY IT LOUD—I'M BLACK
AND I'M PROUD
1967–71

Howard University

My brothers, Cliff and Eugene, were already attending Howard University when I arrived in the fall of 1967. Eugene was a senior, and Cliff was in his second year of law school. While they had an apartment on Third Street NW just down the hill from the main campus, we needed a larger place that would accommodate the three of us. We moved up to Bergamo East, an apartment complex on upper Fourteenth Street NW. It was quite a large apartment with a big enclosed porch that doubled as a bedroom.

Howard was a big change from Hudson Valley. The most distinct change was that virtually everyone was black, including the professors and the administrators. I soon discovered that even the people who looked white were actually part of the Washington, DC, black elite that often set themselves apart from other Negroes. These were people from *successful* Negro families that over the years would only marry people who were of lighter skin and from professional backgrounds. They were referred to in the DC community as "light, bright, and damn near white." There were however, some on campus who rebelled against their upbringing and often could be found looking rather ragged just to show that they were part of the people, meaning, of course, black people.

Politically, we were in the middle of the Vietnam War, and the draft-age youth began to protest against the war. We were also coming to the end of the civil rights movement. Young people began to question the gains made under Dr. King through nonviolence. H. Rap Brown and Stokely Carmichael began to talk about black power—a recognition of not only the power of the Negro in America but also a proud identification of being black. The term *Negro* was relegated to implying a meek and compliant person without self-esteem, and the term *black* implied a strong, proud individual who had self-esteem. The Black Panther Party was on the rise. America's cities—Newark and Detroit—had begun to burn in anger over the socioeconomic and political deprivation that existed in the black community. James Brown, the Godfather of Soul, changed his processed hair to an Afro and released a hit record called, *Say It Loud - I'm Black and I'm Proud.* On campus, we began to seek out our roots. There were many African brothers and sisters on campus. We began to wear dashikis and Afros. For me, this was a transformation of perspective. It took me some time to absorb what was happening. It seemed as if I had grown up overnight and was suddenly confronted with the struggles of all black people in America.

I remember vividly the transformation at Howard. I went to a funeral at the chapel on campus not because I knew the deceased but because I heard that Dr. Mordecai Johnson would be doing the eulogy. He was a preacher and an educator that was known for his great oratory skills. At age thirty-six, he became the first black president of Howard University in 1926 and held that position until 1960. Dr. Johnson was quite elderly at the time, and I wanted to see and hear him while he was still among us. It was the first time I had witnessed a eulogy where the family smiled and laughed. He was masterful. Yet there seemed to be little appreciation on campus for these giants of our past.

Dr. James Madison Nabrit Jr. was president of Howard at the time. He had been part of the civil rights legal team that worked with Thurgood Marshall and others in the 1940s and '50s on many of the lawsuits to win freedoms for black Americans. Now there were protests on campus demanding the resignation of this *Negro* because he was viewed as too compliant with the powers that be. At the time, the vast majority of the students at Howard University received financial aid, and Howard University received a substantial portion of its operating funds from Congress and was constantly faced with threats that they would cut off funds unless the students could be controlled. At the height of discontent and unrest, Howard was shut down and the gates blocked with school furniture. Dr. Nabrit eventually resigned, and James E. Cheek, the then dean of the law school, was named president. I cannot be judgmental about the times. I can say that to the extent we denied the tremendous contributions of the giants who served not only Howard but also all who suffered discrimination in America, we owe them an apology on the one hand and our eternal gratitude on the other.

Making the Grades

I knew that I was at Howard on a shoestring budget. Neither my brothers nor I had any money. We used student loans and worked part-time to remain at Howard. I knew that I had to get some sort of scholarship, or I would not be able to continue. Therefore, I was determined to make the dean's list so that I could qualify for tuition. My first semester turned out to be a disaster. I got four Bs and a C, which resulted in a 2.8 grade point average on a four-point scale. I did not get the scholarship I wanted. The next semester and thereafter, I consistently made the dean's list and finished Howard with a 3.6 grade point average. I also got my scholarships. I continued to work to help pay our rent and buy food and clothing.

Smithsonian Institute

My first job while attending Howard was at the Smithsonian Institute as a night guard. I worked from four o'clock to nine. I got the job by taking a civil service exam. It was my first encounter with the *preference* system that gives preference credits to veterans on examinations. Although I had not served in the military, I nevertheless got a job because I scored a hundred on the exam. Unfortunately, I think one of my superiors knew that I did not have a military background. He seemed to be on my case from the time I arrived at the then history and technology building at Fourteenth Street and Constitution Avenue. It seemed that I could not do anything right even though I did exactly what everyone else did on the job. I needed the job and decided that I was not going to quit. If he wanted me out of there, he would have to fire me. National events during the first half of 1968 overshadowed any issues that I had with my job.

The Assassinations

The first was the assassination of Dr. Martin Luther King. It was about half an hour before closing time when I heard from another guard that Dr. King had been assassinated in Memphis. There was an eerie pall over the face of everyone. Disbelief seemed to hang in the air. It seemed as if it took hours for that half an hour to pass. I wanted to get home. I wanted to hear what happened and what was happening. Everyone changed clothes silently and quickly and then disappeared into the streets in silence.

By the time I got home, the television was filled with reports of anger across the country. The most peaceful man in America had just been violently assassinated! Leaders were on television, pleading for calm. In the middle of his presidential race, Robert Kennedy was asked to comment. His words were intended to be calming, but I had trouble listening. It was only much later that I appreciated what he had to say in a most difficult hour.

The next day as I journeyed to campus, I witnessed a sight that I had never seen before or since. The people were in a trance. They were moving, but they seemed totally stunned and angry. Ironically, the anger forced a camaraderie that had not existed before. Black people were actually showing respect and deference to each other. They were united in their grief and their anger. I continued on to campus only to find that the university had been closed in honor of Dr. King. We were all encouraged to return to the dorms or our homes. By the time I got halfway back home, I could see fires in the distance in downtown Washington. Rioting and looting had begun.

I continued toward home, and the people began to break windows and enter stores that had closed out of respect for Dr. King or out of fear of what was about to take place. Soon the streets were full of people of various ethnicities and more were coming from every direction. Stores were being looted. Contrary to what the media later claimed, there were many cars driven by white people with Maryland and Virginia license plates, and those people wear taking clothing and foodstuffs from stores that no longer had windows or doors. The police completely withdrew from the area. In the distance I saw more fires. By the time I got home, I heard on the news that the military had been called out to protect the government buildings downtown. Later there would be military personnel on every corner and a curfew from four in the afternoon to six in the morning.

The riots in Washington changed the mood in Congress. While the Democrats seemed to respond sympathetically to issues raised by Dr. King, there were still some southern senators who demanded that actions be taken to deal with the lawbreakers. Dr. King had already planned a Poor People's Campaign that would result in a camp along the Reflecting Pool between the Washington Monument and the Lincoln Memorial. Rev. Ralph Abernathy promised that he would continue forward with Dr. King's agenda. He came to Washington, DC, with two mules named Stennis and Eastland, whose namesakes were the two segregationist senators from Mississippi. By this time, President Johnson was being vilified on the national scene because of the war in Vietnam and rendered powerless in Congress, having previously announced his intention not to run for reelection.

Amid this turmoil, two months later Bobby Kennedy was assassinated in Los Angeles. Everyone seemed to be numbed by the news. I was sitting at the table, studying for my exams when I heard that Bobby had been shot in the Ambassador Hotel in Los Angeles. I couldn't believe what I had just heard. When I went in to awaken my brother Eugene to tell him, he thought I was kidding. Sadly, I was not. There were no riots this time in Washington, just numbed disbelief. Nevertheless, underneath the grief there remained the changing mood of black people in America. It seemed as if the pendulum toward civil rights for black people was about to swing in the opposite direction.

Making College Friends

In many ways my experiences at Howard paralleled my life in Albany. I knew people, but I would call very few my friends. For the most part, I got to know the people who were in my classes or those who came over to visit my brothers. I was at a disadvantage in that during my first year at Howard I worked and lived off campus. There wasn't much time to spend making friends. Nonetheless, there was a girl named Linda in my social science class. I couldn't take my eyes off of her. She was smart, quiet, and quite attractive. Everyone seemed to want to get to know her. I just observed from a distance. One day I asked her if she wanted to take a walk with me. She surprised me by saying yes without knowing where we were going.

Linda was a local girl from DC. She had a boyfriend, but things weren't going that well. I said a lot of things to her. I told her that I, too, lived off campus with my brothers and that I worked at the Smithsonian. She seemed impressed. Soon we were sitting next to each other in class, and we often talked after class. I liked her a lot. I asked her to go with me to a concert. She agreed. Little did I know that this would be my first embarrassing moment with her.

Our car was a 1961 black Corvair. Cliff was also going to the concert and agreed to take me to pick up Linda. We got to the concert with no problem. The trip home was the problem. We blew a tire, and we did not have a spare. We also did not have any money. I mean, not one cent! A service station was across the street, and we pushed the car over to the station. I can see myself now saying to Linda, "Do you have $1.50 that I can borrow to fix the tire?" She looked at me, smiled, and said yes. I was floored by her eagerness to help. We took Linda home and laughed all the way back. When we got there, we told Gene and laughed some more. I could not wait to get paid so that I could repay her, and I did.

My next encounter was not so pleasant. I invited Linda to a party at our apartment. This was going to be a dress-up affair. Everyone would be dressed in coats and ties for the men and cocktail dresses for the women. Unfortunately, I didn't own a suit. The only suit I had was a green sharkskin suit once owned by my brother German. It was about five years out of date. I thought that because the apartment would be dimly lit, I could hide in the shadows, and the suit would never be seen in the light of day. Such was not to be. I picked Linda up at her house. I had my coat on and never went inside. At the apartment I took Linda into a bedroom, and we reclined on the bed. Unfortunately, as more people arrived, we needed the bed for the coats. We then came out where everyone else was congregating in the dimly lit room. Then the moment of reckoning came. Linda asked for a drink of water, and I went into the kitchen to get the drink. Linda followed me. She then saw this ugly green suit in with all its warts. She did not say anything. The next day at school, she sat on the other side of the room in her former seat. She left immediately after class, and I was not able to speak to her. I knew then I had blown it with her. She may have thought I was rich, particularly with two other brothers at Howard at the same time. She now knew that I was not. We eventually talked by telephone, and she made it clear that she just wanted to be friends. I was devastated for about a month.

There was another woman in my classes that became one of my best friends—Jeanne Roanne. She was a dark-haired woman with very distinct facial features. Jeanne looked much younger than her years. She always took more than a normal course load of classes and managed to get As in most if not all of them. She was a very bright individual with tremendous drive. I later found out that she was married to a professor at the University of Maryland. Gene and I were invited to a party at her house in Maryland where we met her husband and some of their friends. The problem was that they were old enough to be our parents and sort of ignored us the whole evening.

My second year at Howard, I got a job working in the administration office, where I found out Jean's age. She knew that I knew and appreciated the fact that I did not make a big deal of it. I liked Jeanne a lot and probably developed a romantic attachment to her, but we never let our relationship go in that direction. She was a fun person and a great motivator. She was determined to excel and wanted to be associated with like-minded people. I believe we *fed* each other in this regard. I have not seen or heard from Jean since our graduation.

Tough Times

Some people saw three brothers in college and law school at the same time as unusual. Little did they know or appreciate how unusual it was. Our parents could not afford to help us go to college. We knew we would have to rely on loans, jobs, and scholarships if we could get them. We were determined to succeed, and we knew that we had to help one another. Somehow without ever really discussing it, we pooled our funds to get an apartment, pay the rent, pay the car note, and buy some food. We missed more than a few meals, but we rarely missed class. Many times we had to wait until Cliff got paid from his job on Fridays to buy food.

There came a time when we knew that we would not be able to pay our rent. I remembered that Evelyn Goldstein's sister Lillian had told me that if I ever needed anything, I should call her. I called Lillian and asked her if I could borrow a hundred dollars. She said that she would lend me the money from a family investment club. The club required that you pay the interest in advance at the time of borrowing. This meant that I would receive ninety-five but would have to pay back one hundred. I didn't understand the economics of this transaction. I was just grateful that someone would give me a loan with no collateral. I received the money in time to pay the rent and buy some groceries. Lillian was indeed a true friend. We repaid the loan on time.

My Girl—Maybe Not

I worked in Albany during the summer of 1968. Once again, I was getting serious with Carol (not her real name), a girl I had been dating since high school, although we did not attend the same school. She attended a private school. Carol was a couple of years younger than me. She was my first real girlfriend, and we both were somewhat idealistic in our relationship. We did not smoke, drink, or swear in each other's presence and intentionally did not get too intimate in our relationship. We both thought that one day we would get married.

Carol and I began talking about getting married. We looked at rings at several stores and finally agreed upon one. Carol insisted that I ask her mother about marriage and that I formally propose. I was invited to Carol's house for dinner. I arrived early, and her mother put dinner on the table. We ate the entire meal without discussing the impending proposal. Her mother cleared the dishes and cleaned up the kitchen while Carol and I sat in the living room. Her mother then joined us in the living room and seemed to promptly fall asleep on the couch. I knew then that I would have to make the proposal in front of her mother. It was awkward, but I took out the ring and got on one knee and asked Carol to marry me. She said yes. We then awoke her mother and told her about the proposal. She was not surprised. She just wanted to know if we thought we were prepared for marriage. I told her yes, but the truth was that I wasn't at all sure.

We set the wedding date for the next summer. Later we agreed upon a date in August of 1969. It seems that the summer went by fast, and I soon found myself back in college. Almost immediately, I began to hear rumors about Carol that I had not heard before. Whenever I would mention the rumors to her, she would deny them. I had an oil painting done of myself and sent it to Carol. I wanted her to think about me as much as I was thinking about her. For a time, it seemed to work. We either talked on the telephone or wrote letters often. Carol and a friend paid us an unexpected visit in Washington, DC, that turned out to be quite awkward. Her friend was obviously pregnant, and Carol kept insisting that she wasn't. The school year past quickly, and I was back in Albany for the summer of 1969.

I slowly came to the realization that I needed to confront Carol on the rumors. I knew she would deny them, although I was hoping she would simply tell me the truth. I wanted to believe her. She was very upset when I asked her again about the rumors. I told her that I wanted a relationship based on trust and truth. I knew that I could not marry her if I could not feel that I could trust her completely. She said that if I did not believe her, then perhaps it would be better if we did not get married. The wedding date was about a month away. It was not to be.

Columbia University School of Law

The law school phase of my life actually began in the fall of 1968. I applied to several law schools, including Cornell, Harvard, Yale, and Columbia. Cliff and Eugene were already at Howard University Law School. I wanted to try a different school. I knew that if I went to another law school, I would need to get a scholarship and student aid. My grades and LSAT score were excellent, and I knew I could get recommendations from several professors.

Fortunately for me, Columbia was actually recruiting at Howard that year. The interviewer was rigorous. The interview could not possibly have been the usual kind for the interviewer. Once I told him my major was political science, he seemed hell-bent on finding out exactly how much I knew about the subject. He fired a series of questions at me as if I were being cross-examined. Once it became clear to me that I was being tested, I played the game with him. I deliberately answered his questions in a way that *begged* the next logical question, and he complied. I don't think he ever caught on because he seemed to enjoy the interchange. At the conclusion he said that he was impressed with my knowledge of world political systems.

I received a rejection from Cornell. In the early part of January, I received an acceptance from Columbia with an indication that a financial aid letter would soon follow. Harvard indicated that I was on their wait list. I never heard from Yale. Columbia sent a letter indicating that I would receive a full tuition scholarship and that I would be eligible for certain student loans. I would have to provide the remainder of the required funds for room and board. I decided to wait to hear from Harvard before responding to Columbia.

In the meantime, a friend of mine from Albany (I'll call him Henry) was in the school of engineering at Howard. It was a five-year program that required him to work during his fourth year. He had gotten an internship at Grumman Aircraft on Long Island. He asked if I wanted to get an apartment in New York. I told him that I would go to New York to look around. I had not as yet accepted the offer at Columbia. Neither us knew anything about New York. We got off the bus at the Port of Authority on Eighth Avenue at Fortieth Street. We walked down to the YMCA at Ninth Avenue and Thirty-Fourth Street (I think) to get our rooms. We were careful to watch which streets we took in order to remember how to get back to the Port of Authority.

We began our search by first looking in the newspaper for listings. We did not see anything that we could afford. We decided to walk around the area. Our strategy was that if we stayed in the area, it would be easy for Henry to get to Long Island, and I could take the train up to Columbia too. We found a studio apartment on West Twenty-Fifth Street for $180 a month. Feeling that we had lucked out, we put down a deposit. I don't know what I was thinking about since I had not as yet decided to go to Columbia. We were just happy to have found an apartment. We talked about it all the way back to Albany on the bus the next day.

When I arrived home, there was a letter from Harvard University School of Law. I had been accepted! I was offered scholarship funds but not full tuition. Now I had a dilemma. *Should I go to Harvard and tell Henry that I could not go in on the apartment, or should I accept Columbia's offer?* Henry was my friend. Although I am sure he would have understood if I decided to go to Harvard, I decided that I could not renege on my commitment. I sent my rejection letter to Harvard and my acceptance to Columbia. Had I known then what I subsequently discovered, I am sure I would have made a different decision.

Living with Henry

Eugene and I had known Henry for a long time. We knew his mother and his sisters. They were good friends and good people. The first sign of trouble was when we purchased food. We shopped together and split the cost. Because I had lived with my brothers and we had lived for one and all, it never occurred to me that any guidelines were necessary regarding food. I paid no attention to how much food Henry consumed. I assumed that if we ran out, one or the other of us would buy some more. Then I noticed that Henry was careful to split everything. He never ate more than half of anything. When we bought a package of three pork chops, he would use a ruler to divide the third pork chop! He would divide a pie in half and eat only half of the cookies. His preciseness was driving me crazy! I finally told him that it did not matter to me what he ate or even how much. He said he understood, but he wanted to make sure he was only eating his share.

A few more idiosyncrasies peppered the situation too. Henry had a pair of "Jesus" slippers (thongs), one of which had a broken strap. Rather than fixing the strap, he would drag his feet every time he walked. The constant dragging noise did not seem to bother him at all. I was never more beside myself than when after lending to him the money he needed to pay his part of the rent, he then turned to me and asked, "Do you have your share of the rent?" I do not know why he thought I would lend him money if I did not have the money to pay my rent. I was at wit's end by the time the end of the school year rolled around.

First Year of Law

I did not work my first semester in law school. I wanted to make sure that I could keep up with my courses. I was now at another level of education with another level of colleagues. I didn't know what to expect. I did know that I was going to give it my best shot. Henry and I did not buy desks for the apartment until the second semester. Until then, I used one end of my footlocker trunk to eat on and the other end to study. I usually sat on the floor when studying so that the lamp could shine on the footlocker. There are many times I felt like quitting and getting a job. I would then think about the road I had already traveled and I knew that I had to continue. Sometimes I prayed—first giving thanks and then asking for direction. Things were not always clear to me, but I am sure God was with me. My ultimate frustration was when I had used my last seventeen cents (apart from my tokens to ride the subway to campus) to buy a small box of elbow macaroni. With a little salt and pepper added, it would become my supper. I held the pot over the dishwater in the sink to drain off the water. The pot top slipped, and my supper fell into the dishwater! I dropped to my knees, and tears welled up in my eyes. I had not eaten all day, and my supper was now part of the dishwater. I am not sure when I finally got some money. I am sure that I did not get it from Henry or any of my new friends at school. They never knew my situation. Only God knew. As I look back on those days, I learned to live within my means and to live without. Because of my mother's admonitions in my childhood, I had no desire to beg, borrow, or steal. My only desire was to get beyond the moment. It reminded me of that old gospel "Troubles Don't Last Always."

Letters from Home

I never expected to receive any letters from home. Members of my family did not write letters. So you can imagine my surprise when I received not one, but two letters about a month apart from my mother in the fall of 1969. I knew that although she did not complete her high school education, she did know how to read and write. However, I never saw her write anything other than her name. The first letter was to ask whether I wanted my old Remington typewriter that I had used in college, but did not take with me to law school. She wanted to give it to my nephew Leroy as a Christmas present. Leroy was attending Seton Hall University at the time. The second letter reflected her loneliness and her concern for the grandchildren in her care. She thought that since I had received a student loan for law school, I might be able to help her buy Christmas presents for the grandchildren. Even so, she was careful to emphasize that I should not "cut yourself short." I never shared with her my financial difficulties during my first semester of law school. I sent her some money and asked Cliff and Gene to do the same. Both letters continued to show her love for children even as she struggled with her own well-being. I retain the letters as reminders of her dedication to children.

The Class of 1972

The first-year class was large in several respects. I believe it was the largest law school class to that point in time. It also had the largest number and percentage of woman and the largest number and percentage of black students. The black students in my class were, for the most part, older than me. Frank Bolden, James Perry, Jerry Langley, Clifford Haye, and Charlie Spain had all been in the military with the rank of lieutenant or captain. Neither Vernon Mason nor I had been in the military. Yet we seemed to bond pretty quickly. We all wanted to graduate and become lawyers. We knew that it would not be easy. Most of us had come out of a predominately black school environment. We were contending with the cultural change as well as the academic challenge.

As college graduates and ex-military people in some cases, the black law students were very mature. As such, we took our business seriously. We quickly formed study groups and took advantage of opportunities to share knowledge. I found the relationships extremely valuable. When I look back, I realize that I have not had a similar support group over the years since law school. Ironically, as strong as the bond seemed to have been, we did not maintain it beyond graduation. Occasionally, I will see or hear from someone, but it has not been the same. Perhaps it was only meant to be for that brief period in time.

We sat in alphabetical order so that the professors might easily identify us. As a result, it was easy to get to know the people immediately around you and impossible to know the others unless you happened to work on an assignment together. I thought the classes were challenging for the most part. Professors Reese, Rosenberg, Cover, Uviller, and Sovern were all quite engaging. However, the requirement that you buy the textbooks that were written by the professors oftentimes seemed like a waste, particularly when the course material actually consisted of handouts of other cases not included in the textbooks. I bought a book by Professor Wechsler for my criminal law class. Professor Wechsler was a former prosecutor during the Nuremburg Trials after

World War II. He was also often mentioned as a potential nominee to the US Supreme Court. However, the professor that taught the class spent almost the entire semester on a single case to discuss the essential elements of a crime. The purchase of the Wechsler textbook was a waste of money.

Then there were the professors themselves. I was never quite sure whether the black students were accepted on an equal footing. The younger professors, such as Schmidt and Cover, seemed more receptive than some of the older ones. Indelibly marked in my mind was the occasion when I was called upon by Professor Hans Smit to answer a question. Before I could provide an answer, he interjected that I didn't need to be so "niggardly" with my answer. He obviously tried to express one thing while emphasizing another. Everyone in the room knew what he meant and how he meant it. I took the high road and responded to his question without regard to his choice of words. I could feel the gulp of everyone, and yet I felt the satisfaction of not having stooped to the level of the questioner to make my point.

Getting Ourselves Together

At the end of my first year of law school, I returned to Albany to work on a youth project with my cousin McKinley Jones Jr. My brother Clifford, who got a summer job at the Federal Reserve Bank of New York, had the unpleasant experience of living with Henry. Suffice it to say that he was very happy to see the end of that summer, particularly knowing that Henry would be returning to Howard to finish out his fifth year of engineering school. I returned to New York in time for Henry's departure. My only satisfaction was when we had to decide how to divide up the furniture. He had everything worked out evenly until we came to the coffee table. He could not figure out how to divide it! I told him that I wanted my half of the table. Frankly, I was prepared to let him keep all the furniture except my desk. After a period of torment, I told him that I didn't care how the furniture got divided. It wasn't worth that much to begin with. Based on my experience with Henry, I decided that I would never have a roommate again.

McKinley was a big, dark-skinned man with broad shoulders standing about six feet two inches tall and weighing more than two hundred pounds. He spoke sometimes with a slight stutter but always with authority. He chose his words carefully and usually anchored in his experience and education. He was seven years older than me, and he had spent his earlier years in the military and working for the state of New York. My older brothers, John and German, knew him better than I did. I got to know him shortly before he got married to his wife, Gail. They subsequently had three girls—Michele, Robin, and Kristin. I had begun college, and we often talked about issues around the black community in Albany and in the country as a whole. He made it his business to stay up on the activities of civil rights and black power leaders. However, his primary concern was always about the education of black youth. Too many young people were not going to college, not finishing high school, and either becoming single mothers (girls) or going to reform school or jail (for boys) at a young age. He wanted to change the downward spiral of black youth and instill in them a sense of pride and confidence in themselves.

McKinley and I applied to the Albany County Opportunities, Inc., for a grant to run our youth program in the summer of 1970. It was a particularly difficult time for the black youth in the city because they could not find jobs and they did not have any money or any community activities to keep them focused. We developed educational activities for them featuring black history, poetry, acting, and writing. We called the program "Getting Ourselves Together." We got permission to use

School No. 5

School No. 5, an abandoned school on North Pearl Street adjacent to the Neighborhood House, the local community center. We met with the local youth and some adults to structure evening events, including allowing the youth to decorate the school the way they wanted it to look. In an effort to give the youth responsibility as well as jobs, we put most of them on the payroll at the minimum wage and paid them by the hour for their work in the evenings. We also had dedicated adult staff and volunteers to help oversee the preparation and implementation of the programs. Mrs. Larmond, the grandmother of two of the girls in the program, cooked most of the meals for our special events and was known for her incredible fried chicken.

GOT Youths

Word spread throughout the community, and soon we had about a hundred youth attending our evening programs. The youth felt empowered to express themselves through literature, poetry, theater, and leadership. Our challenge was to harness the energy into self-respect, respect for others, achievement, and discipline.

The youth were being impacted by the black power movement, some of which was being portrayed as encompassing hatred, drugs, and criminal activity. We wanted the youth to develop self-esteem, broaden their education and aspire to lead a positive and productive lifestyle. We saw them as future leaders in the community.

Malcom X

Our leadership did not go unchallenged by the participants. The young adults did not have the historic background to the civil rights movement. They did not grow up in the South. Nor had they actually experienced racial prejudice. They only knew their current condition of deprivation and poverty and accepted the utterances of black power leaders that it was all caused by white oppression. The "by any means necessary" encouragement of black power leaders had an attractive appeal. We were in a constant struggle for the hearts and minds of the youth to process all the thoughts coming their way. Our tactic was to encourage self-respect, respect for the community, and the ability to think for themselves. The key was to allow the youth to take ownership of the program activities and to be held accountable for positive results. It became clear to most of them that reaching consensus requires a willingness to listen to others and to compromise. They learned to properly prepare for the positions they wanted to take and not simply echo the sentiments of others. They also learned the basic fact that being right about your cause did not mean everyone was going to agree with you. By the end of the summer, the youth had an experience that will always be a positive part of their lives.

Hallmark—A New Beginning

For my second year of law school, I moved from the West 25th Street address to 107th Street at Broadway in order to be closer to Columbia at 116th Street and Broadway. This time I had to pay more rent, and I did not have a roommate. The loans from Columbia would not cover my rent and living expenses so I had to find a job. The Columbia Financial Aid Office sent me to Hallmark Cards on 55th Street and Fifth Avenue to interview for a night manager job. I had not managed anyone before and knew very little about the workings of a card shop. Nonetheless, I must have said something they liked because I was offered the job at the end of the interview as night manager during the week and day manager on Saturdays. I accepted.

At Hallmark, except for the day manager and the security guard, all the workers were women in their twenties. Most of these women were also actors working between acting roles on and off Broadway. The customers were predominately upscale shoppers from the Upper East Side of New York. It was not uncommon for prominent New Yorkers and people from the stage and screen to come into Hallmark to purchase cards and accessories. The women employees always had a sharp eye out for them and would get a case of the giggles and stares whenever a celebrity came into the store. The store was an eventful place both day and night.

- Sheila, one of our friendly employees, would not stand at the register, and she insisted on having one of her legs upon the trash can behind the register. One night the position of her leg caused her dress to move upward, and it was obvious that she was not wearing underwear. I told her to put her leg down because we did not want to confuse the customers about what was being sold. It did not seem to bother her.

- Two elderly customers, apparently husband and wife, were looking at cards in the sympathy section. The wife said to the husband, "I am going to get this card for Joyce. I know she would like what it says." The husband said, "She is not dead." The wife said, "I know, but I would like to show her the card I would send when she dies."

- A famous singer and actress called the store to request that we send over an assortment of children's books for her to select some for her children. We explained that we do not provide that service. She responded that she would send someone over for the books and return the ones that she did not want. I said no.

- Two customers came into the store and stood by the candles in the window on Fifth Avenue. They appeared to be engaged in a serious conversation. I noticed that they had a tall package and that it was resting on the floor between them. Having been there for some time, I asked them if I could get someone to help them. One of them said they were waiting for the bus. I looked down and noticed that some candles were missing from their usual location. I asked one of the girls whether we sold any candles, and she said that she did not think so. I went back over to the location and observed that even more candles were missing. I called security. The two customers walked out the door. Apparently, the package they were carrying had a trap door, and they were putting the candles into their package.

Living Uptown

Living closer to campus had its pluses and minuses. As for my apartment at 107th Street and Broadway, the minuses seem to be predominate. My apartment was on the seventh floor just off the elevator. It was a one-bedroom apartment with kitchen and living room areas. I had the essentials—a full-size bed, a kitchen table, a sofa, a black reclining chair, a homemade bookcase, and a stereo. The bedroom had a window that opened onto the fire escape, and the door was metal with a dead bolt lock. The window had a full metal gate that opened from the inside. I could get out, but no one could easily get in.

I do not normally sleep during the day, but one day I got back to the apartment after lunch and decided to take a short nap before going back on campus. I had been asleep until I heard a noise at the door. At first, I thought it was my neighbor and decided that I really did not want any company, so I did not get up. Then I realized that it was not a knock at the door but rather some other kind noise around the door. I got up quietly and moved toward the door when I saw the lock cylinder going around. My heart started to beat fast as I looked through the peephole to observe a middle-aged black man about five foot eight, unshaven and wearing a dirty red and green cap, with a wrench in his hand. My mind was racing as to what to do. *Should I get the hammer and wait for him to enter? Should I call the police? Should I bang on the door? Should I? Should I?* Finally, I banged on the door as hard as I could. The turning of the lock stopped, and the man spoke, "You motherfucka! Why didn't you say you were home? I ain't wasting my fucking time on you."

As calmly and strongly as I could without giving away the chatter in my teeth and weakness in my knees, I responded, "The cops are on their way, and I got something in here for you if you want to come in here before they arrive."

He responded, "Kiss my ass, motherfucka!" I peeped out the door again, and he was just standing there, looking at the door. After about ten minutes, he decided to leave by way of the stairs. I then called the police.

"James, are you okay?" It was my neighbor from across the hall. I opened the door for her. "Are you okay? That was scary. Did you call the police?" I thought to myself, *So many questions now. Where was she when all this stuff was going down?*

"I am fine, Karen. Yes, it was quite a scare," I said. I had hardly finished my reply when the police walked in without knocking followed by the building superintendent. "So what happened here?" one of the policeman said as if he had heard the story many times.

I said, "Some a——hole just tried to rip my lock off and cursed me out for being home."

"Did you get a good look at him?" he asked. I then went through the whole story and the description. Looking at the superintendent, he said, "You'd better get that lock repaired. It looks like it is in pretty bad shape." The superintendent just looked back at the policeman without acknowledging. The policeman then turned to me and said, "Well, we've got your report. We'll let you know if we get any further information. I guess you know that these kinds of break-ins are all too frequent and nearly impossible to track. Have a good night."

The superintendent looked at me with a "don't blame me" face and said, "I'll fix the lock in the morning. Put a chair behind the door tonight." It seemed like in less than a minute, everyone disappeared, and I was right back where I was before Karen knocked on the door.

The next morning, the superintendent showed up at eight thirty with two men to fix the lock. They added a new dead bolt lock and an A-brace lock. This lock included a metal pole at an angle behind the door with a slot in the lock for the upper end of the pole and a slot in the floor for the lower end of the pole. I had never seen such a lock, but the installers were quite certain no one would be able to enter the apartment with this new lock in place.

One day less than a month later, I had been at school since eight in the morning, and it was now close to seven in the evening. Quite tired and hungry, I was glad to put the key in my lock. I was looking forward to talking to Nancy before hitting the books. I stepped inside and tossed my briefcase on the sofa and grabbed the refrigerator handle to see what dinner might look like. It looked like leftover pizza, so I shut the door. I went to the bedroom to change clothes. I flipped the light switch and could not believe my eyes. I froze while a thousand thoughts ran through my mind. Gaining my composure, I attempted to organize some thoughts. There was glass all over my bed from the window that someone had broken. The metal on the gate was bent, but apparently the intruder had given up trying to get the locks open. All I kept thinking was that I could have been in the bed at the time. I cut the light off and backed out of the room and shut the door.

I went down to the basement to the building superintendent and told him what had happened. He listened as I described the situation, but he did not seem surprised or excited. He waited until I finished. Then he said, "The gate held up?" I said yes. He smiled and said, "Fire escapes are a problem. They provide a way out and a way in. If you make the gate so nobody can get in, nobody can get out. What are you going to do?"

I assumed that was not a question for me, so I asked him, "What are you going to do?"

He said, "I can't do nothing tonight. Here's some rope. Tie the doorknob to the stove so if someone does get in the window, they won't be able to get into the other areas of your apartment without waking you up. I'll fix the gate in the morning." I looked at him with a stunned look, and he knew I was stunned. "Look, nothing to call the cops about. They can't do anything. You'll be all right," he said. Then I took the rope and turned away to go upstairs.

I tied the rope between the bedroom doorknob and the gas line on the stove. I called Nancy and told her the story and asked her not to worry. I am sure she was more than concerned. We talked longer than usual. Finally, I said she should get some rest, and I told her I was going to do the same. I did not get any rest, and I later found out that she did not either. I lay on the couch, but I could not sleep or study. I must have dozed off because I did wake up several times. I had the lights on all night.

At six o'clock the next morning, I decided to take a shower. It was awkward in that I left the shower door open in order to see the bedroom door. I remained up, and I tried to study until the superintendent showed up at eight thirty with a new gate in tow. I looked at him, and he looked at me. Then he said, "See, you'll be all right. This is New York. This crap happens all the time. I'll get a glazer over here to put the windows back in for you. Are you going to be here all day?"

"I did not plan on being here all day," I said.

"That's okay. I got a key. I can let them in and lock up afterward," he said.

"No," I almost screamed, "I'll be here, but I want them to get over here now!"

"Hey, buddy, I understand. Just settle down. I'll get this taken care of," he said.

I could only respond, "I am not your buddy!"

When the superintendent left, I called my brother German. He had once shown me a gun, and I wanted to know if he still had it. I told him what had happened, and I said that I wanted to have some protection now. I told him that I would pick it up when I came to Albany to see Nancy. The glazers came over and repaired the window, and the superintendent put a new gate on the window. I kept the rope and tied off the door. I did not sleep in the bedroom again. On the weekend I went to Albany and picked up the gun. I have no idea what type of gun it was. It did take six bullets.

I had never fired a gun before. For some crazy reason, I wanted to practice. I kept pointing it at the wall in the apartment. I figured that the outside wall was brick and the bullet could not pass through. Then I wondered whether it would ricochet in the apartment. Finally, overcome with curiosity, I pulled the trigger. *Boom!* The noise was very loud, and I ducked. There was no ricochet. The bullet was in the wall somewhere, I hoped. Then I got scared because if people heard the noise, maybe they would call the police. I wanted to leave the apartment, but someone might see me and think I was trying to escape. I sat on the couch and started to shake. I finally convinced myself to leave the apartment. I had to take the gun in case someone came into the apartment while I was gone. I did not want an intruder to find the gun.

The gun felt heavier now, and I needed to hide it on me. I put the gun in the front of my belt and put on my loose-fitting coat. All I could think about was that if I got caught with the gun, I would be kicked out of law school and maybe even go to jail since I did not have a license to carry a concealed weapon. I began to get beads of sweat on my forehead. I decided to take a subway ride to nowhere just to clear my head.

I got on the number-two train headed downtown and stood near the door even though there were seats. At the next stop, a policeman boarded the train and stood across from me. All kinds of thoughts started to go through my head. *Does he see the sweat? Can he see the gun under my coat? Should I sit down? What if the gun moves?* My knees began to buckle, and I slid into the seat next to where I was standing. The policeman looked at me and then stared. I looked away at the signs in the subway as if I were reading them. I tried to sit up straight, but my legs would not move. The doors opened at the next stop, and I had a decision to make. Should I stay on or get off. I could not risk trying to walk, so I stayed on the train. So did the policeman. Finally, I decided to stop worrying about the policeman and loosen up a bit. I crossed my legs and pushed myself upright in the seat. The policeman walked to the middle of the car and then to the door. At the next stop, he got off. I gasped for air.

When I got back to the apartment, I called Nancy and told her the story. I said that I would not keep the gun. I was going to give it back to German when I came up to Albany for Christmas. At Christmastime, there I was standing on Broadway between 107th and 108th Street with Christmas presents and the gun in two large Bloomingdale's brown bags. The building superintendent saw me at the curb and said, "How long are you going to be gone?" Without thinking, I said that I would be back on January 2. When I got in the taxi, I thought about his question and about the fact that he never wished me a merry Christmas. I finally dismissed the whole thing and figured I was being too sensitive because of my experiences in the apartment.

It was January 2, and I was back in New York, back to my apartment, and back to school. The only negative was that Nancy was not with me. I pushed the number seven in the elevator and waited for it to progress slowly to the seventh floor. Finally, the elevator stopped, and I opened the door. I could not believe my eyes. The metal door to my apartment had been opened up like a can of vegetables. It was obviously the work of someone with a crowbar. The break-in had to have been quite noisy. Yet it seemed as if I was the only one who had noticed the destruction.

The invincible A-brace lock was easily removed by sticking one's hand through the wrought metal and taking it out of the way. How would anyone know about the A lock? No one had been in my apartment since the last attempted robbery. Inside the apartment, my stereo and clock were missing. Everything else seemed to be there. My books remained on the shelf, and my money that I put in one of them was not taken. Someone had once told me that thieves did not take books.

Here I was standing in the middle of the floor, looking at my apartment. I was roped off from the bedroom. The door had been literally ripped open, and my stuff had been stolen. What a way to welcome the new year. Now I am totally pissed. I looked up, and there was the superintendent at the door. "What happened here?" he said.

"That's the question I have for you," I said.

"I don't know. I just popped up when I saw you get out of the taxi," he said.

I glared at him. "You do not know. Are your deaf? You did not hear this door being gutted open? You just popped up here?"

"Mr. Lipscomb, I know you are upset, but I don't know anything about this. I do not know how it happened or when it happened."

"I don't either!" I retorted. "But I am damn well going to find out."

Once again, the police came and asked their questions. They did not bother to dust for fingerprints or question anyone other than me about the robbery. They made the obligatory promise about a follow-up, but I never heard from them again. Meanwhile, I gave notice to the building owner that I was moving. He mumbled something about my lease was not up and that I would owe them for the balance of the lease term or until they could find another tenant. I told him that I looked forward to seeing the legal complaint and opportunity to respond with the details of my experience in the apartment.

I found a new apartment on 184th Street and Wadsworth Avenue around the corner from a police precinct. In order to get the apartment, I had to give the superintendent a check payable to the landlord for two months' rent, one month's security, and cash equal to one month's rent. After all, this was uptown New York—vigorish had to be paid or you do not get the apartment.

Mississippi Bound

In the fall of 1971, Charles Evers, the brother of the late Medgar Evers, was running for governor of Mississippi as a Republican. This was before the Solid South turned from the Democrat Party to the Republican Party with the subsequent reelection of Richard Nixon in 1972. A notice was posted in law school seeking poll watchers during the election. I volunteered to go to Mississippi to be a poll watcher. Several law schools and local law firms were involved in the effort. We were dispatched to various parts of the state. Four companions and I were sent to a little place in the Delta area near Tippo, Mississippi.

We arrived in the Memphis airport and drove across the border to the house of a local candidate for office. This was rural Mississippi where cotton fields seemed endless and paved roads turned to gravel and then dirt. We stayed at the homes of various local people. We had modest accommodations by New York standards, but they were royal by comparison to much of what we saw in the community. We were happy to have a bed with sheets and to stay in a house with indoor plumbing.

We arrived a couple of days before the election. We spent the first day going around the community, getting to know the polling places and meeting some of the people. The images remain vivid in my memory. Black men and women were being driven around from one field to another in the back of pickup trucks driven by white men. Many of the houses were made of sheet metal and tied together with wire. There were no indoor facilities. Electricity was provided by a single wire in the middle of the ceilings of the houses. Chickens seemed to wander in and out of the houses at will. We arrived at one house at the same time as the owner who was there to collect his three dollars for monthly rent. We were there to remind the occupant to vote in the election and to offer her a ride to the polling place if she needed one.

We were told that the black people of voting age outnumbered the white people of voting age by three to one. It would seem that if blacks were to succeed anywhere in Mississippi, it would be here. All we had to do was to get the people out to vote. Unfortunately, nothing came easy in Mississippi. We began Election Day by going to each polling place and leaving a monitor to watch the polls. We were surprised to also find federal poll watchers at each polling place. This seemed like overkill at first. Little did we know that the federal poll watchers were also from Mississippi.

As we drove around to polling places, I noticed that we were always followed by at least two pickup trucks, each with a shotgun (they called it a "coon gun") in the rear window on a rack. We arrived at one polling place just as a truck drove up with several black men in the back of the truck. The white driver showed them into the polling place and introduced them to the registrars by name. The driver then took each one into the polling booth and *helped* them vote. Apparently, none of them could read or write, and the driver helped them make their mark on the paper ballots. I had no doubt about which candidate they cast their ballots for.

As we arrived at the next polling place, we learned that the poll watcher we had left there, a local man, had gone home. Apparently, he had been frightened by some voters and left. I took his place at that location. The whole matter seemed rather boring at first. People seemed to trickle in. The registrars and the federal poll watchers seemed to be on speaking terms. However, no one spoke to me. As voters came through the door, the registrar would call out the first name of the voter and ask about the family, "Hiya, Paul. How's the missus this morning? C'mon, sign heah." The voter would sign his name and go cast his ballot. After seeing this go on for a spell, it occurred to me that the registrar was not letting the people tell him their names. He was giving them their names. I objected! I asked the registrar to allow the voter to state his or her name first. He looked at me and smiled. I looked at the federal poll watcher to get his assistance. He said nothing. I was dumbfounded. What was I going to do now? I kept talking. I am not sure what I said, but I believe I threatened to sue everyone in the room. I can't imagine what kind of suit that would have been, but the threat seemed to work. Without agreeing with me, the registrar allowed the next voters to state their names first.

The ballots were paper ballots. The polls closed at nine o'clock. It was now time to count the ballots. It was a slow and agonizing process. I had not eaten or drunk anything since I was left at the polls. There was no place for me to go to the bathroom except outside, and I was not about to go outside by myself. I found myself setting up a tabulation sheet to tally the count with the registrar. The registrar would call out the vote, and two people had to verify, including the federal poll watcher. I was not made part of the process, but I could record the result. It took five hours to complete the tally.

Shortly before the completion, my ride showed up with another friend from another polling place. The completed tally showed that the local black candidate lost by a two-to-one margin, and of course, Charles Evers also lost the local vote. We were not surprised. We got into the car and headed to the local candidate's house. In our rearview mirror we could see the headlights of the pickup trucks following us along the dirt road. I was petrified. My head hurt from hunger, and I desperately needed to go to the bathroom. The sight of the house with people waiting in the front yard made me quickly forget my hunger and my desire to go to the bathroom—at least for a moment. Upon arriving at the house, I found myself dancing from one foot to the other to get to the bathroom, trying not to get my clothes wet.

Black American Law Students Association

The Black American Law Students Association had been formed shortly before I arrived at law school. Black law students at predominately white law schools found it necessary to organize so that they could be connected to people at a particular school and also students at other law schools. BALSA was alive and well at Columbia, and all the black students joined. In the fall of 1971, the students elected a new president of BALSA from the first-year class. The newer students were determined to have their voices heard on black issues, and they seemed to see most things as *black* and *white*. My class, being a bit more mature, did not see black issues only by color but rather as issues in need of solutions that accounted for the presence of black people.

The new BALSA president was popular and well-liked by his peers until it became known that he was married to a white woman. Many but not all of his classmates felt that he had deceived them or at the very least that he should have told them. Some wanted him to resign, so the president resigned. As a result, a special election was held to elect a new president. I was asked to run for the office, and I agreed. I made a short presentation to all the BALSA members. I made it clear that BALSA needed to speak with one voice and to focus on the issues of importance. I told them that while it may have been important to some members of BALSA to know before electing the previous president that he was married to a white person, the fact in and of itself was irrelevant to whether he could be a good president for BALSA. I was not present for the deliberations, and I do not know what my opponent from the first-year class said to the members of BALSA. I was, however, elected as president of BALSA.

As president, I had a number of issues to deal with, including securing on-campus space for BALSA and pressing the administration for the appointment of black teachers. Shortly after I became president of BALSA, Dean Sovern announced the appointment of Kellis Parker, a black law professor, to the faculty for the coming year. BALSA had been strongly advocating the appointment of a black faculty member, but they had not been consulted on this appointment. Dean Sovern lauded Mr. Parker's credentials, which were stellar. However, I chastised Dean Sovern for making the appointment without consulting or informing BALSA. This was another instance growing out of the sixties whereby black people and their organizations were tolerated but were not respected by the establishment. We were supposed to be overjoyed by the appointment and not see the fact that our opinion did not matter.

There were two women law students who seemed to be constantly looking for things to complain about. They seemed to have captivated the freshman class but not anyone else. In an effort to assure them that all views would be heard, I agreed to have dinner with them and others at the apartment of one of the women. I thought I would be meeting with a small group to discuss issues.

I rang the doorbell, and she buzzed me in to the building. When I reached her door, I knocked, and she opened the door. "Good evening, Mary (not her real name). How are you?"

She responded, "Come on in. I am just finishing up with making our dinner. I won't be but just a minute. Would you like a glass of wine?"

I responded somewhat quizzically, "Yeah! Where is everyone?"

"It will be just us," she said.

Not knowing whether that meant others were invited but not coming or that they were never invited, I said, "Everyone has a busy night?"

"No," she said. "I thought it would be best if we got to know each other." My heart skipped a beat. I was not sure what she meant by her comment, and I needed an exit.

Mary returned to the room with the glass of white wine in hand and offered it to me. I accepted and continued to stand. She said, "Have a seat. Dinner will be ready in a minute." I sat down, still thinking about an exit plan. None was readily apparent. Mary returned from the kitchen with two plates in hand and placed them on the table. Soon she was adding Cornish hens and vegetables to the plate and filling the wineglasses. The food was excellent, and the conversation was light. It seemed like a short time had passed, and we had finished the main course.

Mary arose from the table and took the plates with her. She turned on music from somewhere in the apartment and asked me to go sit in the living room area. I thought she was putting dishes in the sink, but it seemed like she was taking a rather long time. She soon emerged in a red velvet pajama top and matching short pajama bottoms with a pink pom-pom on the rear end. I nearly jumped up and ran, but I held my composure. I was not going to do what I think she wanted. As I began to speak, her telephone rang, and she picked it up. I do not know who was on the telephone, but she did not hang up right away. After about ten minutes of her still talking on the phone, I tapped her on the shoulder and said, "Thanks for dinner, but I've got to go. I will see you tomorrow." Without waiting for an answer, I turned and opened the door and left.

The next day I saw her in the BALSA office, and with her head down, she said, "You're dirty." I did not respond. Actually, I felt pretty clean.

Will You Marry Me?

I had met Nancy Moore in the summer of 1969 at the First Reformed Church in Albany at Clinton Square. She was working in a youth program there, and I was working with my cousin McKinley Jones Jr. in a youth program that was using the church facilities. I was just rebounding from Carol, and I didn't want to become immediately involved in a relationship. Nonetheless, I enjoyed talking to Nancy, and after I started law school in New York, we started to talk a lot on the telephone. She was working as an instructor at Hudson Valley Community College's Urban Center in Albany. The next summer I worked in a summer program with my cousin McKinley during the day, and she got me a job teaching mathematics at night at the Urban Center. For me, teaching was all about the money. However, I grew to appreciate over the summer how much my adult students wanted to improve upon their education in order to have a better life. It became a life-changing experience for me and for the students.

Nancy is the oldest of four children born to Willard "Bill" Moore and Norma Kathryn "Kay" DeFreese in Hillburn, New York. Her siblings are Daria, Willard Jr., and Christopher. Bill was one of fourteen children born to Harvey Moore and Nancy Whitlow of Tuskegee, Alabama. Kay was one of ten children born to Harry DeFreese and Mary Adelia Van Dunk of Hillburn, New York. Kay's family heritage was Dutch and Ramapo Indian. Bill and Kay met while serving in the military during World War II, and they married during the war. Bill worked as a mechanical engineer on construction equipment, and Kay worked off and on at the local school. The Moores moved from Hillburn to Pine Bush, New York, where Nancy and her siblings graduated from Pine Bush High School. After graduation Nancy went to the State University of New York at Albany, where she graduated with a bachelor's degree of arts and science. Nancy continued her education at SUNY Albany and subsequently received her master's degree in special education.

Having spent most of the summer of 1970 working and socializing together, Nancy and I were in a serious relationship by the end of the summer when I returned to law school. When we did not visit each other, we would always call. Nancy soon got to meet some of my law school friends at various gatherings when she was in New York.

The years 1970 and 1971 proved to be the years of weddings. At least four of my BALSA classmates were married. It seemed as if I was attending one bachelor party after another followed by one wedding reception after another with the same people. It was not until the summer of 1971 that I decided to ask Nancy to marry me. I would have asked her sooner; however, I was flat broke, and I did not know what type of life we would have if I were not working and had a lot of bills to pay. However, as I talked to her more and more, it seemed that we were both committed to the common goal of achievement. Thus, when I finished my second year of law school and started to work at the Urban Development Corporation in New York City as a summer intern, I used my first paycheck to put a deposit on a ring. I recall having to guess at the ring size, but the person who helped me in the store assured me that I could come in later with Nancy to get the proper size.

August was upon us, and I still had not asked the most important question of my life. I didn't know what she would say or for that matter, what I would say. I came over to her apartment on Hamilton Street in Albany one evening to have dinner. After dinner we sat down to watch TV, but before she could turn the TV on, I said, "Nancy, will you marry me?" She looked at me somewhat startled and then realized that I was serious. She said yes. The conversation got a little crazy after that, and we both were just talking to fill in the time. When we stopped, she called her mother, and they talked on the telephone for a while.

I know she was surprised when I asked her to marry me. I was surprised when she said we should get married right away. Since I had to return to law school, we agreed upon the Saturday after Thanksgiving. Although I had to return to law school and she had to work, it seemed like we were planning the wedding every day. We decided to limit the guests to family and a few of our friends from law school. Nancy asked her sister Daria Holcomb to be her maid of honor, and I asked my cousin McKinley to be my best man. Nancy asked Rev. Samuel R. Holder, a longtime family friend, to perform the wedding at his church in Queens, New York, and the reception was to be held at Nancy's aunt Jean and uncle Robert's house in Patterson, New Jersey.

My wedding day arrived, and I was getting a few butterflies in my stomach. It was an overcast day with the threat of rain. I did not have much to do, but I wanted everything to be perfect. I wanted to make sure my mother and father would be able to come down from Albany, but my father was too ill to travel. McKinley assured me that he would bring my mother down to the wedding. My mother was going to stay at my apartment. Nancy and I had a suite reserved at the Inn Towne Motor Hotel on the west side of Manhattan near Forty-Second Street. There would be no immediate honeymoon. Nancy was returning to Albany to work, and I was going to continue my third year of law school on Monday morning. We would spend the next six months living apart.

Everything did go well. McKinley came down with his wife, Gail, and my mother. My mother had insisted on attending the wedding of her youngest son even though she was not well at the time. I was happy for her presence and she was even more so for Nancy and me. Everyone arrived at the Dunton Presbyterian Church in South Ozone Park, New York, on time. Friends from law school, Hilburn, and Albany were already at the church. Nancy arrived shortly after my arrival and the front doors of the church were opened by the ushers. There in the arch of the doorway stood Nancy and her father. As I looked down the aisle, I could only see Nancy in her wedding gown, and she was looking back at me. She was beautiful and graceful as she stepped slowly toward me. I became nervous and prayed that I would not stutter when saying my vows. Soon Bill Moore was offering me the hand of his daughter and Nancy and I turned to face Rev. Holder. The tension was broken when Bobby Wilson, one of my Albany friends, started to hiccup and continued to do so throughout the ceremony. After a while, it caused everyone to giggle. When we said our vows, the hiccups synchronized in the background, but Nancy and I were oblivious to them as we spoke to each other.

"Nancy, I promise with God's help to be your faithful husband, to love and serve you as Christ commands as long as we both shall live," I said.

"James, I promise with God's help to be your faithful wife, to love and serve you as Christ commands as long as we both shall live," she said.

Reverend Holder held our hands and said to the people in attendance, "I present to you James and Nancy Lipscomb, husband and wife!"

A New Beginning

EPILOGUE

In Coeymans, New York, the place of my birth, there was a sense of community where all the Negro people knew the struggle. At the center of life was the church—Riverview Missionary Baptist Church. These were God-fearing people who often spoke with reverence for the power of the Holy Spirit to bring peace in the times of trouble and comfort in times of despair. We yearned for a better life that only God could bring. One day we would all have shoes and sing with great joy in the presence of the Lord. We would sing an old gospel song called "I Got Shoes."

I got shoes. You got shoes.
All of God's children got shoes.
When I get to heaven, gonna put on my shoes,
Gonna walk all over God's heaven, heaven, heaven.

Everybody's talkin' 'bout heaven, and I'm going there,
heaven, heaven.
Gonna walk all over God's heaven.

This book has been about the first twenty-five years of my life, which serve as the foundation for the remainder of my days. Coeymans is where the seeds of my faith were sown. I have tried to live out the American dream, and I've realized along the way that my salvation has been an ever-present reality that transcends my dreams. As I look back through the years, I see more clearly than ever the tender hand of God's mercy and His grace not only in my life but also in the lives of others. I have grown in my worldly understanding of the song from that of merely overcoming poverty, racism, and the adversities of life to my spiritual understanding, namely that of overcoming self-pity, selfishness, envy, and pride. Today I am a humble man who's so filled with *joy* that I am able to stand on the words of the apostle Paul to the Philippians. "I have learned to be content whatever the circumstance. I know what it was to be in need, and I know what it was to have plenty. I have learned the secret of being content in every situation, whether well fed or hungry, whether I am living in plenty or in want. I can do everything through Him who gives me strength" (Philippians 4:12–13).

ABOUT THE AUTHOR

James L. Lipscomb

James Lipscomb is a former executive vice president and general counsel of a Fortune 40 public company.

His civic affiliations include serving as chairman of the Citizens Budget Commission of New York, chairman of the Citizens Housing and Planning Council of New York, trustee of the Practicing Law Institute, director of Graffiti Ministries, Inc., and a member of the Economic Club of New York.

Lipscomb received an AAS degree from Hudson Valley Community College, a BA degree (*cum laude*) from Howard University, a JD degree from the Columbia University School of Law, and an LLM (corporations) degree from the New York University School of Law. He has been admitted to practice law in New York, California, federal courts, and the US Supreme Court. Throughout his career Lipscomb held leadership positions in various local, state, and national legal organizations, including the American College of Real Estate Lawyers, the State Bar of California and the Association of the Bar of the City of New York. Lipscomb, known for his willingness to speak truth to power, has received numerous awards and accolades in recognition of his achievements, including being named to *Inside Counsel* magazine's 2006 list of the top fifty most influential in-house counsel members in North America.

Like his mother, Lipscomb has dedicated time and resources to help children in need. In 2004, Lipscomb cofounded the Center of Hope (Haiti), Inc., a Connecticut nonprofit corporation for the purpose of developing and operating an orphanage and school in Hinche, Haiti. The orphanage provides a home for orphaned children, and the school educates the poorest of poor children who would not otherwise be able to go to school. Learn more at www.centerofhope-haiti.org.